Soraya believes:
You are magical.
You are mystical.
You are spiritual.

Soraya became known as Scotland's favourite psychic when she predicted a huge win for someone who, three months later, won 2.8 million in the National Lottery!

She is a respected Reiki Master and teaches Reiki to the medical profession as well as to private students.

In addition, Soraya is featured regularly in local and national newspapers, on radio and TV, such as the BBC's *Heaven and Earth Show,* and was resident astrologer for *The Sunday Post*. She is also an avid and renowned numerologist.

She is mother to three children, Ian, Claire and Tori; grandmother to Ashi, Jack and Eva; and wife of artist Martin Conway.

www.soraya.co.uk

SORAYA

enhance your
Psychic Powers

SORAYA

enhance your
PSYCHIC POWERS

GEDDES & GROSSET

Published 2005 by Geddes & Grosset, David Dale House,
New Lanark, ML11 9DJ

Copyright © 2005 Soraya

Additional material © Geddes & Grosset
Fortune cookie illustration by Mark Mechan

First printed 2005

ISBN 1 84205 105 9

Printed and bound in Poland

POLSKABOOK

Contents

Exercises in Divination 43

Appendices

Introduction

The chances are that if you have been drawn to pick up this book you have had experiences that may have lead you to believe that you might be – even just the tiniest bit – psychic. Well, the good news is that you are right. We are all psychic.

I am sure you will have had the experience of standing in a crowded room and feeling as though someone is staring at you. You try to remain casual, despite a slight creepy feeling, as you turn and look around, and there across the room looking right at you is an old friend, grinning from ear to ear. Instantly, you forget your initial apprehension and you probably spend the next ten minutes laughing about your mutual experience. I say mutual because when your friend relates his or her side of the story they will probably tell you that they have been watching you for ages – willing you to turn around.

Coincidence or psychic experience?

You are thinking of someone you haven't seen for ages and 'ping!' an email arrives from them or the phone rings. 'I was just thinking about you!' you say.

Psychic: the *Collins English Dictionary* defines this as 'outside the possibilities defined by natural laws as mental telepathy' or 'sensitive to forces not recognised by natural laws' and 'a person who is sensitive to parapsychological forces or influences'.

Yet how can having psychic powers be outside natural laws when it is the most natural thing in the world? We cannot explain it and so in scientific terms it becomes unnatural – how typical of our times, when we expect everything to be explained by science.

My interpretation of a psychic is someone who is sensitive to the vibrations around them, seen or unseen. You are unable to touch your psychic instincts, or explain them in scientific terms but to deny them or say that they are outside natural laws is like denying animal instincts; the wolf's need to howl at the moon, the bird's need to migrate, the adult salmon's need to return to the river where it was conceived.

You know that you have instincts, but the sad thing is that most people have forgotten how to use them. Have you ever been confined to bed after an illness or an operation and found that the first time you try to walk again your legs are like jelly? It's almost as though you have forgotten how to walk.

It's the same with your psychic ability. If you don't use it, you begin to forget how. All you have to do now is practise every day, at every opportunity, and soon, just like walking again after an illness, you regain full strength.

I often hear people asking me whether I am psychic or clairvoyant. My initial response is usually to ask them if they know the difference and more often than not they don't. Clairvoyance, from the French, means to see clearly, to see things beyond the limits of what we imagine our five senses can perceive. A clairvoyant believes they can foretell the future through divination. A psychic is sensitive to the energies around them. They are both (mostly unused) talents that can be retrieved through practice and meditation.

The collective name for any form of seeing into the future is 'divination' and there are many ways to do this which are listed in this book. But, before you can even begin, you must be able to tune in to your higher self. In the following chapters are exercises to optimise your sensitivity to the energies around you and achieve this link with your higher self.

This may demand new skills that are presently unfamiliar to you. Perhaps you will have heard of some of the terms that you are about to read about before, but were unaware of what they meant.

All will become clear.

Chakras

Learning About Your Chakras

The simplest way to explain chakras is to describe them as energy power points within your body. We have twenty-one minor chakras and seven major chakras within our bodies. In this book we will be focusing on the latter. Each chakra has its own specific location, traditional name, common name, colour and function, as shown in the illustration. This will be a fairly brief description to give you a working base but should you wish to expand on this subject, there are many specialist books on chakras.

The Source of Infinity Above

The chakra which connects you to the source of infinity above is situated approximately twenty-four inches above your head, more specifically, at the end of your fingertips when you have your arm stretched high above you. The colour of this chakra is brilliant white. Its function is to make the connection between you and the energy from infinity.

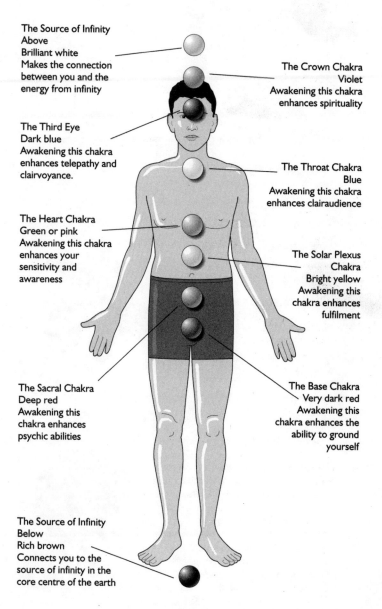

The Source of Infinity
Above
Brilliant white
Makes the connection
between you and the
energy from infinity

The Crown Chakra
Violet
Awakening this chakra
enhances spirituality

The Third Eye
Dark blue
Awakening this chakra
enhances telepathy and
clairvoyance.

The Throat Chakra
Blue
Awakening this chakra
enhances clairaudience

The Heart Chakra
Green or pink
Awakening this chakra
enhances your
sensitivity and
awareness

The Solar Plexus
Chakra
Bright yellow
Awakening this
chakra enhances
fulfilment

The Sacral Chakra
Deep red
Awakening this
chakra enhances
psychic abilities

The Base Chakra
Very dark red
Awakening this
chakra enhances the
ability to ground
yourself

The Source of Infinity
Below
Rich brown
Connects you to the
source of infinity in the
core centre of the earth

The Crown Chakra

Most people think of the crown chakra as the first chakra. It is situated at the top of your head.
The traditional name is *Sahasrara*.
The colour is violet.
The associated flower is the lotus.
The associated crystal is clear quartz crystal (double pointed where possible).
Awakening this chakra enhances spirituality.

The Third Eye Chakra

The third eye is situated in the middle of the forehead between the eyebrows.
The traditional name is *Ajna*.
The colour is very dark blue.
The associated flower is the orchid.
The associated crystal is lapis
Awakening this chakra enhances telepathy and clairvoyance.

Throat Chakra

The throat chakra is situated in the throat and governs the mouth, ears and nose.
The traditional name is *Vishuddha*.
The colour is blue.
The associated flower is the cornflower.
The associated crystal is turquoise.
Awakening this chakra enhances clairaudience (the ability to hear sounds beyond the range of normal hearing).

The Heart Chakra

The heart chakra is situated in the heart and is
the centre of unconditional love.
The traditional name is *Anahata*.
The colour is green or pink.
The associated flower is the rose.
The associated crystal is rose quartz.
Awakening this chakra enhances your
sensitivity and awareness to all things.

The Solar Plexus Chakra

The solar plexus chakra is situated in your
upper abdomen, just beneath your rib cage.
The traditional name is *Manipura*.
The colour is bright yellow.
The associated flower is the sunflower.
The associated crystal is sunstone or citrine.
Awakening this chakra enhances fulfilment.

The Sacral Chakra

The sacral chakra is positioned on the
abdomen, just below your navel and just
above the pubic bone.
The traditional name is *Swadisthana*.
The colour is deep red.
The associated flower is the poppy.
The associated crystal is carnelian or moonstone.
Awakening this chakra enhances psychic abilities.

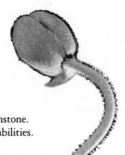

The Base Chakra

The base chakra is positioned at the base of the spine.
The traditional name is *Muladhara*.
The colour is very dark red.
The associated plant is the roots of the lotus or a tree.
The associated crystal is obsidian.
Awakening this chakra enhances the ability to ground yourself.

The Source of Infinity Below

This chakra connects you to the source of infinity in the core centre of the earth and is situated approximately twenty-four inches below your feet.
The colour is rich brown.
The associated plant is the roots of your favourite tree.
The associated crystal is clear quartz.

When performing any kind of spiritual work it is important that you are connected to the source of infinity above and below.

Memorising the Chakras

Once you are familiar with the location and function of each of the major chakra points you can begin to practise opening your chakras. I can almost hear you asking 'Why would I want to do this?' That's like saying: 'I have a nice car but I keep it in the garage because I don't drive'.

Your chakras are the unseen power centres that stimulate or suppress your energy. Closed or asleep they suppress your energy, while opened and awake they stimulate it.

Memorising the Chakras

At this point it would be useful to make your own chakra cards. Take nine pieces of card and draw, depending on your artistic ability, either a circle or a flower. You could draw the flower that is associated with the chakra. With coloured pencils, paint or felt tips colour each circle or flower with the colour which relates to each chakra. Underneath add the details about the charkas, the traditional names and their popular names.

Take the chakra cards and, if you have them, the appropriate crystals and lay them out in a straight line. This will help you imagine or visualise what being connected looks like.

Gather the cards, mix them, and then turn them over and again lay them in the correct order. Do this several times until you get the sequence correct. Do not tire yourself out or you will become disheartened. The traditional names can be difficult to pronounce so, as

Memorising the Chakras

you work with each card, try to focus on the common name, the colour and the function. For example, for the crown chakra, the colour is violet and the flower is the lotus. Practise in this way until you feel as though you know all the chakras, their functions and their colours, then you will be ready to move on to the next exercise.

Learning How to Relax

Being able to relax is crucial to becoming receptive to the energies around you. The first lesson in learning how to relax is discovering how to make yourself unavailable to telephone calls or visits from friends and family. You only need thirty minutes in the day or evening when you can switch off the phone and tell your loved ones not to disturb you, unless of course it is an emergency. You can practise in your bath or on your bed, your favourite chair or even the floor if you prefer it.

Once the phone has been switched off, make yourself warm and comfortable and begin to breathe slowly and deeply. Close your eyes and listen to the sound of each breath as it fills your lungs and then listen to the sound each breath makes as you breathe out.

Try to visualise each breath in as being brilliant white and healing. Don't panic if you think you can't visualise – you can imagine instead. There is a difference. Imagining happens in your crown chakra, whilst visualising happens in your third eye, but I will explain more of this in the following pages.

As you breathe out visualise that you are breathing out all the negative energy from your body. Maintain this steady flow of watching positive healing energy filling your body and negative energy leaving your

Visualisation

body. Gradually you will be filled with a sense of calm and peace but after a short while your logical side will try to take over and the distractions will begin.

At this point all manner of things can pop in and out of your mind, which is frustrating. It's called 'monkey brain' and the cure is simple. Go back to visualising positive energy flowing into your body and when a distracting thought comes in send it to the back of your head and again focus on your breathing. Each time a distracting thought occurs send it to the back of your brain.

Practise this relaxation technique as often as you can and soon you will be ready for the next step.

Visualisation Exercise

Make yourself comfortable. Close your eyes and begin to breathe in positive energy as before. When you feel relaxed and your breathing is slow and steady, focus all your attention on your third eye.

Remember your third eye is the space between your eyebrows in the middle of your forehead. Imagine that inwardly you are looking at that space. Sometimes the image of an eye will appear. Don't worry, this is normal. Many people tell me that they can see the eye but nothing else.

The secret here is, when you see your third eye look right through it. At first you may only see a black or dark space but gradually images may begin to appear. Do not try to force this, just remain relaxed and focused and then when the images do come all you have to do is observe them. As you become more comfortable and familiar with this technique you may hear or have the impression of hearing sounds, words, and even music. Sometimes you may want to focus on a particular theme and 'monkey brain' continually distracts you. The following exercises will help you to maintain your focus.

Focus Exercise One

Aim: An exercise to establish an image that will help focus your mind and prevent thoughts wandering to the everyday.

Make yourself comfortable. Close your eyes and begin to breathe in positive energy as before. When you feel relaxed and your breathing is slow and steady, focus all your attention on your third eye.

Visualise an apple pip before you. The skin of the apple pip is dark brown and shiny. In your mind's eye, turn the seed around so that you can look at it from all angles. The moment that you begin to feel distracted focus again on the apple pip and begin to see a tiny little green shoot appearing at the top of it. The shoot begins to grow, and there before your eyes it has produced two tiny leaves. It grows taller, gaining in strength until it is a young tree. As the leaves begin to mature you can see buds forming which burst into bloom. As the apple blossom begins to fade the fruit begins to grow. There before you is an apple. It is red and juicy and ripe for picking. In your mind's eye you pick the apple and begin to eat the fruit. Be aware of the sweetness of the fruit and the feeling of the flesh and juice in your mouth. Soon you are down to the core and all you are left with is the apple pip.

Spend a few moments focusing again on the apple pip and then gradually come back into yourself. Stretch your legs and arms, take a deep breath of positive energy and open your eyes.

Focus Exercise Two

Aim: An exercise practising the abilities you developed, and the image that you focused on, in exercise one. You are learning to focus on that image every time a distraction pops into your head.

Make yourself comfortable. Close your eyes and begin to breathe in positive energy as before. When you feel relaxed and your breathing is slow and steady, focus all your attention on your third eye.

See again before you the apple pip but this time do not allow it to grow. You may look at it from many angles but always try to stay with the apple pip as it is. Any time that a distracting thought comes into your mind discard it and return to the picture of the apple pip. Practise this exercise until you can stay with the apple pip for at least ten minutes. When you have finished, gradually come back into yourself. Stretch your legs and arms, take a deep breath of positive energy and open your eyes.

Focus Exercise Three

Aim: Trying to lengthen the time which can be spent focusing the mind and to leave the mind open to new images.

Make yourself comfortable, close your eyes and begin to breathe in positive energy as before. When you feel relaxed and your breathing is slow and steady, focus all your attention on your third eye. Again, see before you the apple pip. This time remove the apple pip from the picture and focus on the space that the pip has left. Each time that a distracting thought occurs send it to the back of your mind and again focus on the space that the apple pip occupied. Try to maintain your focus on this for at least ten minutes. Gradually come back into yourself, stretch your legs and arms, take a deep breath of positive energy and open your eyes.

Practise this exercise every day until you can maintain your focus on the empty space, and soon you will be ready for the next exercise.

Focus Exercise Four

Aim: To create the state of mind in yourself in which psychic images come to the fore.

Make yourself comfortable, close your eyes and begin to breathe in positive energy as before. When you feel relaxed and your breathing is slow and steady, focus all your attention on your third eye. Look into the same space that the apple pip occupied and this time allow images to flow freely. Do not allow thoughts to distract you but maintain your attention on the space. Do not become disheartened if nothing happens for a while. Everyone is different and will make progress at a different rate. Gradually, with daily practice, images will begin to appear and all you have to do is observe. These images may mean nothing at all and it can almost feel as though you are watching a video. Sometimes unpleasant images appear. Discard these immediately and return to the last pleasing image. You are always in control here and it is important to remember this. Do this exercise for ten to fifteen minutes and when you have finished stretch your legs and arms, take a deep breath of positive energy and open your eyes.

Opening Your Chakras

Chakras take in and give out energy. Opening your chakras leaves you more receptive to the energies around you. You must also read the exercise on closing your chakras which immediately follows.

This next part is best done lying down on your bed, sofa or even the floor. I prefer the floor because I can surround the area on which I am going to be lying with crystals. Disconnect the telephone and prepare your surroundings so that you can be completely comfortable.

Lie down in the space that you have prepared and begin to breathe slowly and deeply. With each inward breath visualise positive energy filling your body and the space that you are lying in. Visualise a pure, brilliant white light about a foot above your head and allow this light to flow down from infinity above you into the top of your head.

As this pure light from above touches you, visualise that it is touching a lotus bud. Allow the colour to change from white to violet and see the lotus being blessed from above and awakening. Petal by petal the lotus blossom begins to open until this flower covers the entire top of your head. In the centre of the lotus is a swirling ball of energy. This is the core centre of your intelligence and your spirituality. Blessed by the light, the flower opens, so too does your spirituality.

The light from above travels further down and rests upon your third eye in the middle of your forehead between your eyebrows. Touched by the light and the love from above, the colour begins to change into a very dark blue. You begin to see an orchid. Visualise it as just a bud, asleep and waiting to be awakened. As it is touched by the light, the orchid begins to bloom and open. In the centre of the orchid is a swirling ball of energy. This is the core centre of your ability to create and see your future before you. When the orchid opens, it awakens your third eye chakra and stimulates telepathy and clairvoyance.

The light from above travels further down and rests upon your heart. As this pure light from above touches your heart, visualise the colour beginning to change to the colour pink and a rose bud waiting to be awakened. As it is touched by the light, the rose bud begins to bloom and open into the most beautiful rose that you have ever seen. In the centre of the rose is a swirling ball of energy. This is the core centre of your ability to feel. As the rose opens, it awakens your heart chakra and stimulates your sensitivity and love, bringing awareness to all things, increasing your psychic power and your ability to instinctively know and understand.

Further down, the light from above travels and enters the middle of your body. As this pure light from above touches your centre, visualise the colour beginning to change to yellow and then into the bud of a giant sunflower. As it is touched by the light, the sunflower begins to bloom and open. In the centre of the sunflower is a swirling ball of energy. This is the core centre of your

Opening Your Chakras

power. As the sunflower opens, it awakens your solar plexus chakra and stimulates your strength and determination, helping you to achieve fulfilment.

The light from above travels further down and enters the lower part of your body just above your pubic bone. As this pure light from above touches this area, visualise the colour beginning to change to red and then into the bud of a poppy. As the poppy is touched by the light, it begins to bloom and open. In the centre of the poppy is a swirling ball of energy. This is the core centre of your psychic power. As the poppy opens, it awakens your ability to respond to psychic stimulus.

Further down, the light from above travels and enters the base of your spine. As this pure light from above touches your base, visualise the colour beginning to change to very dark red and the roots of a giant tree. As the light touches the roots they begin to come to life. In the centre of these roots lies a swirling ball of energy. This is the core centre of your ability to ground yourself and remain connected to the earth below. Visualise these roots travelling down through your hips, your thighs, your legs and through your feet to the source of infinity below. As the roots touch infinity below they begin to hold on and draw nourishment and healing up into your body.

Visualise your body as being filled with all the colours in the rainbow and as these colours swirl around your body they will heal and re-energise both your physical and spiritual life.

Relax and enjoy the experience and fill your heart, mind

and spirit with peace, love and joy. See in your mind's eye each of your chakras as open and active.

Everyone has a guardian angel, sent by the great spirit to accompany us on our journey through life – good times and bad times. Visualise your guardian angel approaching you carrying a purple cloak. This cloak will protect you from negative energy. Allow your guardian angel to wrap the cloak of protection around you. Once this is done it is time for you to come back into the here and now.

Take a deep breath, stretch your arms and legs, and slowly, in your own time, open your eyes. Do not jump up and start hurrying around. Take things slowly and easily. Make yourself a cup of tea and relax. Some people feel light headed after this type of exercise. If you experience this eat something that is made from ingredients grown in the earth, like a potato scone or a packet of crisps, rather than something which comes from the branches above the earth, like an apple, or something made from wheat like bread or crackers.

Practise this exercise every morning or evening and gradually you will find that it takes less and less time to open your chakras. Soon opening your chakras will be like switching on a light. When you can do this – and only then – you will be ready to move on to other exercises.

Closing Your Chakras

Closing your chakras is as important as opening them because they pick up the energy that is around you. Perhaps you have been meditating in the morning before

Closing Your Chakras

you go to work. Feeling good inside and out, you go to work and when you get there the atmosphere is hostile because of some event. There are angry faces and voices everywhere you go, and people full of moans and groans. This drains your energy and makes you feel angry or miserable too. Drawing a purple cloak of protection around you at the end of a meditation will help to ward off these negative energies, keeping your energy field pure and unbroken. Closing down your chakras will do this too but you must remember to open them again when the energy around you is better.

To close your chakras, find a comfortable place to sit, switch on your light from infinity above you and as it touches your crown chakra see the flower closing, petal by petal, until it once again becomes a bud. Repeat this process until you come to your heart chakra. Allow this chakra to remain open. Keeping your heart chakra opened will allow you to maintain pure loving thoughts regarding any negative situation or person you might encounter.

Move down through the remaining chakras closing each one until you come to your base chakra. As you reach this chakra visualise your roots drawing back up into a tight ball at the base of your spine. Closing your base chakra will help to prevent you from becoming depressed by a negative situation.

After a bad day go and sit or lie down in your favourite place and perform your chakra opening exercise once more, and visualise peace and harmony flowing through all your chakras.

Meditation

Crystal Meditation

You will need at least eight crystals for this exercise and they can be of any size or colour. If you are just beginning to collect crystals the most common and easy to obtain are clear quartz, amethyst, rose quartz and citrine, although the Crystal List in this book will help you make your selection for specific purposes.

Prepare an area where you can lie down and have your chosen crystals to hand. Have a glass of water or fresh fruit juice and a small snack nearby. When everything is ready, place one crystal just above where your head will be when you are lying down. Place another just below your feet. Position one crystal where you will be able to reach it by your left side and another by your right side. Holding the remaining crystals in your hand, lie down and place a crystal on your forehead just above and between your eyebrows. Position another on your throat. Place one crystal on your heart and another on your solar plexus. Pick up the crystals that are by your hands and hold them throughout the following meditation.

Make yourself comfortable, close your eyes, and begin to breath in positive energy. When you feel relaxed and your breathing is slow and steady, focus all your attention on the crystal that is in the position above your head. See

Crystal Meditation

this crystal filling with bright, positive, sparkling energy and as it fills and overflows allow that energy to move down through the top of your head to meet with the crystal that is situated between your eyebrows. As before, see it filling with bright, positive energy and as it begins to overflow allow it to trickle down through your chest to the crystal that is over your heart. This crystal will also begin to fill and overflow with bright, sparkling energy and as it does so allow it to trickle down to the crystal on your solar plexus. Allow this crystal to fill and expand with energy and as it overflows it will move down through your body to connect with the crystal at your feet and across to the crystals in each hand. Now see your entire being vibrate with pure, sparkling energy and allow this energy to expand outwards to fill your surroundings. When you have reached this state it is time to ask your guardian angel to step forward.

Close your eyes and visualise your guardian angel forming before you. Imagine a smiling, loving, being surrounding you with protective light. When you see your guardian angel ask for his or her protection or advice or whatever it is that you wish to know, for example:

'Guardian Angel (use his or her name if you know it), friend and protector, with your love I know that I am not alone in this world. With love and respect I humbly ask that you come forward. I ask for your help as I seek answers and ask you to protect and guide me. Please surround me with your light. Thank you for your constant presence and unquestioning love.'

Spend some time in quiet meditation with your guardian angel and, when you are ready, give thanks and gradually begin to come back to yourself. Visualise all the sparkling energy being locked into your body.

Visualise a protective cloak being placed round your shoulders and see roots emerging from the base of your spine and travelling down through your body into the ground beneath you. Say these words: 'I am now ready to come back to myself feeling refreshed, revitalised and confident.' Gradually curl and relax your toes and muscles, and when you are ready, open your eyes. Gradually sit up, take a sip of water and enjoy your prepared snack. Do not hurry your movements. Instead, take your time and, when you are ready to stand, do so slowly.

Music Meditation

Choose your favourite piece of music – something that really moves or stimulates you. I find that shamanic chanting, pan pipes, native American and Japanese music or wolf and dolphin sounds can take me into quite deep and interesting places. Listen to your chosen piece of music and become familiar with it.

When you are comfortable with all the variations and subtleties of it and are happy with your choice, prepare an area to lie down on and have a glass of water or fresh fruit juice and a small snack nearby.

When you have everything ready, sit or lie down and make yourself comfortable, switch on your music and begin to breathe in a slow, steady fashion. As you breathe in visualise bright light energy flowing into your body and as you breathe out breathe away negative energy. Feel the music and allow it to take you wherever you want to go. Drift free with the sounds and vibrations. When the music has ended, gradually begin to come back to yourself. Visualise all the sparkling energy being locked into your body.

Visualise a protective cloak being placed round your shoulders and see roots emerging from the base of your spine and travelling down through your body into the ground beneath you. Say these words: 'I am now ready to come back to myself feeling refreshed, revitalised and confident.' Gradually curl and relax your toes and muscles and, when you are ready, open your eyes. Gradually sit up. Take a sip of water and enjoy your prepared snack. Do not hurry your movements. Instead take your time and, when you are ready to stand, do so slowly.

Candle Meditation

Your main priority when working with candle meditations should be safety. Make sure that there is nothing nearby that can be set alight and that the candle is secure in a holder. Candles can be purchased in many colours so choose one appropriate to your desires.

White signifies purity, cleansing and knowledge.
Red signifies passion, excitement and action.
Pink signifies love and romance.

Orange signifies strength, power and courage.

Yellow signifies energy, vitality and motivation.

Green signifies healing, growth and fertility.

Blue signifies tranquillity and peace.

Purple signifies protection, meditation and spirituality.

Turquoise signifies communication, protection and travel.

Black signifies grounding and dispelling negative energies.

Candle Meditation One

Choose the colour of candle that you wish to work with and secure it into a holder, remembering to keep it away from any flammable objects or surfaces. Prepare an area where you can sit quietly and comfortably. Do not have any music playing. Have a glass of water or fresh fruit juice and a small snack nearby. When you have everything ready, light your candle, make yourself comfortable and relax.

Fix your focus on the flame of the candle and begin to breathe in a slow, steady fashion. As you breathe in visualise bright light energy flowing into your body and as you breathe out expel negative energy. Keep your eyes focused on the candle and gradually your vision will begin to distort. Do not try to refocus. You may feel as though your eyes are very heavy but maintain this fixed stare at the flame of the candle. If you are naturally gifted or if you have been practising enough, pictures will gradually begin to form in the flame.

Candle Meditation

Follow the movement and colours of the flame and try to stay with this meditation for at least ten minutes. When you are ready to stop and come back to yourself you can begin to visualise sparkling energy being locked into your body.

Visualise a protective cloak being placed round your shoulders and see roots emerging from the base of your spine and travelling down through your body into the ground beneath you. Say these words: 'I am now ready to come back to myself feeling refreshed, revitalised and confident.' Gradually curl and relax your toes and muscles and, when you are ready, open your eyes. Gradually sit up, take a sip of water and enjoy your prepared snack. Do not hurry your movements. Instead, take your time and when you are ready to stand do so slowly.

Always remember to do this after any meditation and if you feel lightheaded remember to eat something. Afterwards you may want to make a note of the time and date, and write down anything you saw or felt that you want to remember. This will also give you something to refer back to later if you realise that you been given advance notice of something.

Candle Meditation Two

Choose the colour of candle that you wish to work with and secure it into a holder, remembering to keep it away from any flammable objects or surfaces. Prepare an area where you can sit quietly and comfortably. This time you can play some music and, as before, have a glass of water or fresh fruit juice and a small snack nearby. When you have everything ready, switch on your music, light your candle, make yourself comfortable and relax. Fix your focus on the flame of the candle and begin to breathe in a slow steady fashion.

As you breathe in visualise bright light energy flowing into your body and as you breathe out expel negative energy. Keep your eyes focused on the candle and gradually your vision will begin to distort. Do not try to refocus. You may feel as though your eyes are very heavy but maintain this fixed stare at the flame of the candle. You may begin to realise that the flame of the candle moves in time with the music and the flame may grow and diminish with the beat. The more upbeat the tempo the more active the flame will become. As you watch focus your mind on the candle and try to communicate with the flame.

See the flame stretching and then in your mind tell the candle flame to grow smaller. Pictures may form and all you have to do is watch and try to remember everything that you see. Follow the movement and colours of the flame and try to stay with this meditation for at least ten minutes. As you become more experienced with meditation you can increase this time but do so gradually. When you are ready to stop and come back to yourself you can begin to visualise sparkling energy being locked into your body.

Visualise a protective cloak being placed round your

shoulders and see roots emerging from the base of your spine and travelling down through your body into the ground beneath you. Say these words: 'I am now ready to come back to myself feeling refreshed, revitalised and confident.' Gradually curl and relax your toes and muscles and, when you are ready, open your eyes. Gradually sit up. Take a sip of water and enjoy your prepared snack. Do not hurry your movements. Instead take your time and when you are ready to stand do so slowly. Afterwards make a note of the time and date, and write down anything you saw or felt that you want to remember.

Third Eye Meditation
Exercise One

Prepare your meditation area and for this first third eye meditation work in silence. Have a glass of water or fresh fruit juice and a small snack nearby. When you have everything ready, make yourself comfortable and relax. Breathe in a slow steady fashion. As you breathe in visualise bright light energy flowing into your body and as you breathe out expel negative energy. Bring light energy down through all your chakras and fill your entire being with sparkling light. When you are completely and totally relaxed focus all your attention on your third eye which is in the space just above and between your eyebrows. Do not be alarmed if you suddenly see an eye. It is yours. This is your third eye and all you have to do now is stare straight into it and through it. At first you

Third Eye Meditation

might see nothing at all except an empty space. This is not unusual. Be patient and practise this as often as you are comfortable with and gradually pictures may begin to form. When you are ready to stop and come back to yourself you can begin to visualise sparkling energy being locked into your body. Visualise a protective cloak being placed round your shoulders and see roots emerging from the base of your spine and travelling down through your body into the ground beneath you. Say these words: 'I am now ready to come back to myself feeling refreshed, revitalised and confident.' Gradually curl and relax your toes and muscles and, when you are ready, open your eyes. Gradually sit up and take a sip of water and enjoy your prepared snack. Remember not to hurry your movements and, when you are ready, slowly get up. Afterwards make a note of the time and date and write down anything that you saw or felt that you want to remember.

Exercise Two

Prepare your meditation area, choose some ambient music, have a glass of water or fresh fruit juice and a small snack nearby. When you have everything ready, make yourself comfortable and relax. Breathe in a slow, steady fashion. As you breathe in visualise bright light energy flowing into your body and as you breathe out expel negative energy. Bring light energy down through all your chakras and fill your entire being with sparkling light. When you are totally relaxed focus all your

Third Eye Meditation

attention on your third eye in the space just above and between your eyebrows. Look deep into your third eye, and be patient. Gradually pictures may begin to form. As before, when you are ready to stop and come back to yourself you can begin to visualise sparkling energy being locked into your body. Visualise a protective cloak being placed round your shoulders and see roots emerging from the base of your spine and travelling down through your body into the ground beneath you. Say these words: 'I am now ready to come back to myself feeling refreshed, revitalised and confident.' Gradually curl and relax your toes and muscles and, when you are ready, open your eyes. Gradually sit up, take a sip of water and enjoy your prepared snack. Remember not to hurry your movements and, when you are ready, slowly get up. Afterwards make a note of the time and date and write down anything that you saw or felt that you want to remember.

Exercises in Divination

In the following list you may find several exercises that you are already familiar with and some that you feel drawn to. Remember to trust your instincts. We are all different and some of us are good at one thing while others are good at something else.

Once you have become familiar with practising various meditation techniques you will begin to realise that you can very quickly attain a meditative state. This is the frame of mind and being that is required to begin to see into the future by any chosen method, whether it be playing cards, Tarot cards, dice or anything else.

As with any new skill, practice is the key to improvement. Do your meditaion exercises as often as possible,and try as many of these divination exercises as you can.

Aeromancy
Cloud Divination

Aeromancy simply means telling the future based on the formation of the clouds in the sky. I am sure there have been times in your life when you have seen faces or recognisable shapes in the formations of the clouds and not paid any particular attention except perhaps to say to a friend 'Look at that.' Wouldn't it be wonderful if you could actually 'read' the clouds?

Aeromancy Divination Exercise

Place a comfortable chair by a window where you can see the sky or, better still, on a fine day sit in the garden, your local park or somewhere in the countryside.

Begin to breathe slowly and deeply and visualise sparkling light moving through all your chakras. When you are completely relaxed look at the various formations of the clouds and choose the cloud pattern that you want to work with. Once you have selected one, stare at these clouds and become aware of the patterns and shapes that they show you.

Each time you see a shape that can be identified stop and make a note of it. Later you can look up the interpretations section in this book and make notes on what you think you are being told. Each time you make an entry into your notebook include the time and the date. After a few weeks you can look back over your notes to see if your interpretations are accurate.

Ailuromancy
Cat Divination

Ailuromancy is all about cats. We are all familiar with the legendary 'lucky black cat' and most cat owners know that these creatures can be very sensitive. One of the most characteristic things about cats is probably their independence. When my daughter Tori was young we went to an animal rescue centre to give a home to a cat. We called him Hassan. He was very handsome with his shiny black coat. Later, when he grew fat and we realised that he was having kittens, he became Hassani and then Ani for short. One day Tori said to me: 'This cat has got to go.'

When I looked over at Tori she was stroking and loving Ani while the cat completely ignored her. 'We have had this cat for eighteen months and she has never shown me any sign of affection,' said Tori. That's what cats are like. They are capable of loving you and purring all over you but only when it suits them. This is one of the reasons that the cat represents independence and freedom. In ancient Egypt the cat was worshipped. The goddess Basset is portrayed as a woman with a cat's head, sometimes with a litter of kittens. For this reason she is known as the protector of pregnant women. In spite of this, many mothers and grandmothers re-home their cats when a baby is due fearing that the cat might suffocate their baby.

Most witches love cats and consider them to be their 'familiar' (spirit guide) although in some cultures they are considered to be unlucky. There are several sayings associated with cats. For instance some say that a black cat crossing your path or coming to visit your home will bring you luck. A cat following you is believed to indicate that money will come to you before the week is out. Be wary of a stranger in the home that your cat hides from. A stranger in your home to whom your cat is attracted is safe. If your cat is staring out of the window, a letter, call or visitor should arrive.

Ailuromancy Divination Exercise

For the next few weeks pay close attention to your cat and its behaviour. Rather than just thinking of your cat as your pet, think of it as your guide. When your cat is in its resting place, unplug the telephone, light a candle and place the candle between you and your cat. Sit in your most comfortable chair opposite your cat and begin to relax. Think of the cat sitting on your lap and see yourself stroking it. In your mind tell your cat how comfortable it would be to sit on your lap. Visualise your cat stretching, getting up and coming over to you. Do not speak or move – just concentrate. Practise this exercise for about five to ten minutes every day. Gradually your cat will begin to realise that you are communicating with it and it will come to you. Sometimes you may need to visualise tempting pictures for your cat to come. Its favourite food, perhaps a can of tuna fish, something that you know your cat cannot resist. When your cat finally gets the message give it a reward and make a fuss of it. Once you have mastered this art of communicating silently with your cat, you can begin to work on a more serious level, especially problem solving or decision-making.

Alectryomancy
Divination Using a Bird and Bird Seeds

Birds could be said to symbolise our own 'flights of fancy'. Who wouldn't love to be able to fly? The saying 'free as a bird' reflects the desire of humans to be able to do this. In many cultures the bird can symbolise thoughts and dreams, even the human soul. Fortune telling by birds could be used in instances where you need to ask questions about hopes, dreams, aspirations and wishes.

Letters of the alphabet, or possible outcomes, are written on pieces of paper and placed on the floor. Birdseeds are then scattered over the pieces of paper and the bird is allowed to peck at the seeds. Whenever the bird pecks at a seed on a piece of paper the letter is noted and soon the answers are found. Be respectful to the bird and thank it.

Alectryomancy Divination Exercise

Traditionally a hen would be used for this exercise but unless you live near a farm, the chickens you are most likely to have easy access to will be in the freezer section of Asda, and this is not suitable! However, if you know someone who has a pet bird you could try this form of divination with their pet if they, and the bird, will allow you.

Prepare an area of the floor and lay out pieces of paper on which are written letters of the alphabet, and one slip of paper with the word 'yes', one slip of paper with the word 'no' and one slip of paper with the word 'maybe'.

Alectryomancy

You could alternatively write possible outcomes and then place all your papers in a circle on the floor ready to receive your prophetic bird. Scatter some birdseed over the papers. Before you introduce the bird to the exercise spend a few moments focusing on the area and visualising positive energy filling the space. Ask your question and then set the bird down in the space and take note of which letters or answers are uncovered or pecked at in the order that they are 'chosen'.

If you know a nice place by a pond or loch where wild birds come to feed you could do exactly the same exercise. Don't choose a windy day though or you may lose all your pieces of paper and be fined for littering the area!

Aleuromancy
Fortune cookies

When my husband and I got married we got my granddaughter Ashie to give all the guests fortune cookies instead of favours and everyone opened their cookies right away to read their fortunes. Traditionally these biscuits were used to hide secret messages and were distributed by the patriotic revolutionary Chu Yuan-Chang in disguise as a Taoist priest.

During the American gold rush and the railway boom the Chinese '69ers were building the great American railway lines through the Sierra Nevada to California. They put happy messages inside biscuits to exchange at the moon festival, instead of cakes, and so the tradition of fortune cookies began. The Chinese settled in San Francisco and a cottage industry in fortune cookies emerged.

Aleuromancy Divination Exercise

Before you begin this exercise why not make your own fortune cookies? You can vary the messages that you put inside and do not forget to include yes and no answers. You could even include a full set of rune symbols (see entry for runes), drawing one symbol per piece of paper and using one per biscuit. Before you begin to make your cookies, write your messages on small, thin rectangular strips of paper and have them close to hand. Each message must be folded into the baked biscuit while they are still hot otherwise the cookies will crumble and break.

You will need the following ingredients:
1 egg white
$^1/_4$ cup/1 oz (28g) of caster sugar
$^1/_4$ cup/ 1 oz/ (28g) of flour
1 tbsp water
$^1/_4$ cup/ 1 oz/ (28g) of melted butter
$^1/_4$ tsp salt
$^1/_8$ tsp vanilla extract
Makes around 6 cookies.

Prepare some paper 'fortunes', around 5 cm long (2 inches), to place inside your cookies. Preheat the oven to 400°F/200°C/gas mark 6. Grease and lightly flour two flat baking trays. Put the egg white and sugar in a small bowl and mix till foamy but not stiff. Mix in the flour with a little water if necessary and add the melted butter, vanilla and salt and mix well. At this point it would be best to let the batter rest for around an hour.

After the batter has rested, place 1 tbsp of the mixture on the baking tray for each cookie; they should be around 6 cm (3 inches) in diameter. Using the back of a spoon, swirl the drops around until the cookies are spread very thin. Only bake one or two at a time because you need to work very quickly, but prepare your next tray while the others are cooking. Now bake for five minutes, or until lightly browned on the edges. Remove the cookies from the oven and quickly, while they are still hot, remove from the tray with a spatula and place upside down on a wooden surface. Put a fortune in the middle of the cookie and fold each cookie in half, across the width of the fortune and seal the edges as best, and as quickly, as you can, trying to make sure that the sides of the cookie puff outwards. Then in the opposite direction pinch the two corners towards each other (but not touching) across the fold to make that familiar crescent shape.

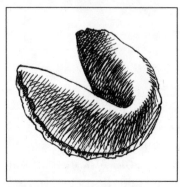

You could place the cookie over the edge of a glass or a cup to help you with this as you guide each pointed corner downwards. Allow the biscuits to cool in small drinking glasses or egg cup trays so that they keep their shape. Keep them in an airtight container.

Alternatively, if this is too fiddly for you (and believe me it is fiddly!) fortune cookies are fairly cheap to buy, especially if you get them from a specialist Chinese supermarket. But, I like the idea of having your own personal messages inside, so it's worth a try.

Each morning or last thing at night before you get ready for bed sit quietly and meditate on the day's events. Focus your mind and ask one question, then put your hand into your fortune cookie jar and choose one cookie. Break it open and read the answer to your question. Make notes in your diary of your questions and the answers you are given and later you can look back and see how accurate you were.

Apantomancy
Chance Meetings With Animals

Many years ago when my children were very small, an interesting incident occurred while we were driving along the main dual carriageway into Edinburgh. The traffic was heavy and moving slowly and about 50 yards ahead of us we noticed that a flock of sparrows were feeding on some discarded food. Suddenly a sparrow hawk flew past us about six inches above the pavement and swooped straight into the feeding sparrows. We were all yelling at each other excitedly, 'Look at that, look at that!' As we drew alongside we were able to see that the sparrow hawk had successfully pinned a sparrow beneath his talons. He shrouded his prey with his wings and looked defiantly at the passing cars.

This would be described as Apantomancy, a chance meeting with animals. I pondered on this event for a long time afterwards and wondered what message was being given to me by chancing upon a bird of prey in the middle of a busy city. I wondered if maybe the message was not for me but was meant for someone else travelling along the same road, witnessing the same sight. Strangely, however, it was on my return from this trip that I discovered I was pregnant with my long-awaited third child Tori. On this occasion the hawk did indeed foretell of a message that brings enlightenment.

Apantomancy Divination Exercise

It is not possible to engineer a divination exercise for this subject but you should pay attention from now on

Apantomancy

to all chance encounters with creatures in the animal kingdom and always make a note of the circumstances. You may not always understand at the time what the event means but referring to your notes later will help you to learn and be more aware as your experience grows.

Arithmomancy
Numerology (ALSO SEE SEPARATE ENTRY)

This is my favourite form of divination and I use it all the time. To me arithmomancy, or numerology, is my first language and every day I am aware of the significance of the numbers that are associated with that day or those numbers that I come across during the course of my work or leisure.

When working with numerology you need only to be concerned with the numbers one to nine, unless of course you plan to make a lifetime study of the subject.

- One is the number of leadership, new beginnings, new ideas and inspiration. The number one will show exciting new changes ahead.
- Two is the number of tact and diplomacy, balance and harmony. Be prepared for some surprises if the number two is significant.
- Three is the number of pregnancy and nursing or nurturing. Socialising, having good times with friends and joining clubs, societies or organisations will be relevant.
- Four is the number of security, assets and the home. Major changes around the home such as repairs, renovations and renewals can be expected, or visits from older males. Four is a very dependable number.
- Five is a number signifying keys that will unlock the answers to your questions or the door to your new home. It is the number that shows the problem areas in your life or any conflict that will be experienced. It is also linked to uniforms of any description.

- Six is the number of tenderness, compassion and difficult choices that have to be made, of crossroads being reached and the eternal triangle. Whereas five highlights the problem, six is the number that provides the solution.
- Seven is the number of control, and questioning comes in here. Control cannot be obtained without full knowledge of all facts surrounding you. With inner questioning, you can then resume control in your life.
- Eight is the number of strength, determination and stubbornness. This number will show that you or someone close to you will have to be very stubborn to achieve cherished goals.
- Nine is the number of completion, seeing the light at the end of the tunnel, or finding your way after stumbling around in the dark. It signifies difficult tasks being completed.

Arithmomancy Divination Exercise

Write a question on a piece of paper and write the numbers one to nine on separate sheets of paper. Mix the numbered pieces of paper and place them face down in a circle on the floor or on a table and put your question face up in the middle. Place both hands with palms facing downwards over the papers and focus all your attention on the question that you have written. Relax and concentrate. When you are ready, choose at random three numbered pieces of paper. Turn them over and look at the numbers.

Think about how you feel about the numbers that you have chosen or what, if anything, these numbers remind you of. Spend a few minutes doing this and then add all the numbers together until you achieve a single number. That will be the answer to your question.

For example, imagine your question had been, 'Will my finances improve?' and your choice of numbers was two, four and eight. If you were born on one of these dates then you would consider your choice to be favourable since most people consider their birth number to be their lucky number. (To calculate your birth number see page 98.) Then you would look at each number independently.

Two is the number of tact and diplomacy, balance and harmony. Be prepared for some surprises if the number two is significant.

This could be an indication that you must balance your accounts and avoid unnecessary expenditure.

Four is the number of security, assets and the home. Major changes around the home such as repairs, renovations, and renewals can be expected or visits from older males. Four is a very dependable number.

I would be inclined to take this as an indication that you are on the right track and that you should concentrate on developing your assets rather than frivolous spending. There may also be some domestic expenses ahead that you will have to be prepared for, hence the advice given by the two should be heeded.

Eight is the number of strength, determination and stubbornness. This number will show that you or someone close to you will have to be very stubborn to achieve cherished goals.

This is self-explanatory and is clearly telling you that you must persevere with a strict budget to generate the improvements that you desire.

Now the fun begins: add the numbers two, four, and eight together and we have the total fourteen. Fourteen is made up of one and four.

One is the number of leadership, new beginnings, new ideas and inspiration. The number one will show exciting new changes ahead.

Four is the number of security, assets and the home. Major changes around the home such as repairs, renovations and renewals can be expected or visits from older males. Four is a very dependable number.

Add these two numbers together and we have the number five.

Five is the number representing keys, which will unlock the answers to your questions or the door to your new home. Five is the number that shows the problem areas in your life or any conflict that will be experienced. It is also linked with uniforms of any description.

I would interpret this answer as being linked to property or expenses associated with property. However, the one and the four show me that you will soon find a new form of financial security which will come to you through changes in or around your present home, provided that you are sensible and stick to a reasonable budget.

Astragyromancy
Divination Using Dice

For this form of divination you can use as many or as few dice as you like and then refer to the interpretations on the numerology list, but, generally speaking, two, three or four dice are best.

Astragyromancy Divination Exercise

Write a question on a piece of paper and place your written question face up in the middle of your table. Place both hands, palms facing downwards, over the question and focus all your attention on the question. Once again, relax and concentrate. When you are ready throw your dice. Remember to pay attention to any numbers that are particularly significant to you. Think about how you feel about the numbers that you have thrown and what, if anything, these numbers remind you of. Spend a few minutes doing this and then add all the numbers together until you achieve a single number. That will be the answer to your question.

Bibliomancy
Divination Using Books

For this form of divination you would think of a question or problem and then choose a favourite book, the Bible or a dictionary. Then, using a variety of methods, you randomly select a passage or word in the hope that this produces an answer or a clue to an answer. If you would like to try this form of divination there are many inspirational books, such as the *Little Book of Fortune, Little Book of Calm* and *Words of Wisdom,* and books about guardian angels on the market. Alternatively, you can use a favourite book of mine by one of my favourite authors, Richard Bach. He says in his book *Illusions*:

'You are never given a wish without also being given the power to make it true. You may have to work for it, however.'

'There is no such thing as a problem without a gift for you in its hands. You seek problems because you need their gifts.'

'What the caterpillar calls the end of the world, the Master calls a butterfly.'

In another of his books entitled *Jonathan Livingston Seagull,* the character of the same name is one of a flock of seagulls who cares less about scrounging for food, and more about mastering the art of flying, than the other gulls. Jonathan Livingston Seagull loves to experience the thrill and exhilaration of flying faster and more dangerously than any gull has flown before. More often than not he crashes, but he always gets up, gives himself a good shake and begins again. The other birds are furious with him and don't understand why he does this. The elders have a meeting and declare him an outcast. In this little book Jonathan Livingston Seagull says: 'When you come to the edge of all the light you have known, and are about to step out into darkness, faith is knowing one of two things will happen, there will be something to stand on, or you will be taught to fly.'

If this has whetted your appetite for more then perhaps Bibliomancy is for you.

Bibliomancy Divination Exercise One

First choose the book that you are going to work with. Make it one that holds a certain significance for you. Then make yourself comfortable in a chair or under a tree, somewhere that you will not be disturbed. Follow your own pattern of breathing and relax, allowing yourself to drift deeply into your question or problem. Keep your chosen book in your hands whilst doing this and after some time, when you feel as though you are ready, randomly open your book and begin to read. You should find your answer or something that helps you to find your answer.

Bibliomancy Divination Exercise Two

Choose the book that you are going to be working with but this time you will need a pencil too. Follow the above relaxation exercise but this time when you open your book keep your eyes closed and use the pencil to mark the part that has your answer. Don't use a pen or you will not be able to rub out the mark that you have made.

Botanomancy
Divination Using Burning Branches and Leaves

This aspect of divination is entirely dependent on whether you have a garden and if you are permitted to burn garden refuse in your area. If this is permitted, the next time that you are having a clear out in the garden and you make a bonfire to clear away all the dead branches you will be able to read the signs in the sparks and the smoke created by the fire. Even the smell that is given can serve to remind you of things or trigger an inner knowledge.

Botanomancy Divination Exercise

For this exercise it is important to depend on your intuition and instincts. Before you begin, select the pieces of tree branches that are going to be used for answering your questions. Remember that the branches or twigs have at some time come from a living plant and proper respect and reverence should be shown. Also you will be using the element of fire and respect should be used here too. A verse to use could be:

Fire engulfing plant and tree,
Grant answers in your flames for me.
To these branches here alight
I ask my questions here tonight.

Alternatively, it would be a nice personal touch if you wrote your own verse.

Set the branches alight and sit in front of the flames, allowing your thoughts to drift over your current

Botanomancy

problems or questions. Use a notepad to jot down anything that you see or feel and always make sure that your fire is safe. You should never leave a fire unattended. Ideally you should allow the fire to go out of its own accord, but if you cannot, before the fire is extinguished thank the elements for assisting you and then smother the flames.

Capnomancy
Divination Using Smoke

This is similar to Botanomancy, but with Capnomancy you can use smoke from any burning source. A bonfire or a hearth fire will do nicely and all you have to do is sit in front of your chosen fire.

Capnomancy Divination Exercise

Be comfortable and relaxed and, as before, allow your gaze to blur whilst in your mind focus on the issues concerning you. It is also fine to just let your mind drift. As images come try to remember them so that you can make a note of them when you are done.

Cartomancy
Divination Using Playing Cards

In a deck of playing cards there are fifty-two cards made up of four suits – Wands, Cups, Diamonds and Swords. Each suit has cards numbered one to ten and then there are three Royal cards, the Jack, Queen and King. Most people are unaware that ordinary playing cards actually origninated from the set of seventy-eight Tarot cards. When it became dangerous to be found with Tarot cards, due to the threat of imprisonment and/or death, the scholars of the Tarot concealed the four Knights of the Tarot and the twenty-two Major Arcana, or Trump cards, leaving fifty-two cards of four suits. These suits were then identified as the ordinary playing cards, which we know today. Spades in Tarot are known as Wands, Hearts are referred to as Cups, Diamonds are known as Pentacles, and Clubs are known as Swords. It should be noted at this point that some people prefer to relate Clubs to Wands and Spades to Swords.

This equivalence shows how it is possible to read ordinary playing cards. However, the reading cannot be truly accurate because the Major cards, which show the changes caused by destiny, are missing and only the effects can be shown. Therefore only part of the story can be told.

Cartomancy Divination Exercise
to Answer One Question

Find a quiet place to sit with a work surface to put your

cards on. Make sure that you will not be disturbed and make yourself comfortable. Have your cards and a notepad handy and put the date and time on the top of your page. Next write your question and sit quietly thinking of this question. While you are doing so hold your playing cards in both hands. Spread the cards face down in front of you and choose one card. You can then look to the following interpretations and write down in your notepad the card and the interpretation given. Also write down any feelings that you have pertaining to this.

When you have finished you should thank the higher energies for helping you. Later, when the problem or situation has reached a conclusion, refer back to your notes and write down the outcome as it developed and any circumstances surrounding the outcome or the lead up to it.

Cartomancy Divination Exercise
for General Guidance

Find a quiet place to sit with a work surface to put your cards on. Make sure that you will not be disturbed and make yourself comfortable. Have your cards and a notepad handy and put the date and time on the top of your page. Next write 'General Guidance' on the page and then sit quietly thinking of your life as it is and how you would like it to be or of any issues that concern you. While you are doing so hold your playing cards face down in both hands. Count out five cards and put these five cards to the bottom of the deck and the sixth card to one side. Count out five cards and as before put these five cards to the bottom of the deck and the sixth card on top of your first 'sixth card'. Continue to do this until you have six cards in your pile. Now turn over your pile of six cards.

The first card relates to your life up till now.
The second card relates to your present circumstances.
The third card relates to your immediate future.
The fourth card relates to your future circumstances.
The fifth card relates to your objective.
The sixth card relates to the influences that will be present.

You can then look to the following interpretations and write down in your notepad the card and the interpretation given. Also write down any feelings that you have pertaining to this.

When you have finished thank the higher energies for helping you. Later, when the problem or situation has reached a conclusion, refer back to your notes and write down the outcome as it developed and any circumstances surrounding the outcome or the lead up to it.

Short Interpretations of Ordinary Playing Cards

Spades (Wands in the Tarot deck)

The suit of Spades, which is associated with the element of Air, tells you about things that you have on your mind and refers to the season of spring.

Ace of Spades – this will be a fertile period in your life.

Two of Spades – you will make a short journey.

Three of Spades – you will plan for your future.

Four of Spades – you will be more content than you have been in recent times.

Five of Spades – quarrels and confusion will upset you.

Six of Spades – you will hear news that will be to your advantage.

Seven of Spades – stick to your principles.

Eight of Spades – you will make several journeys in the near future.

Nine of Spades – you will feel worn out and wonder if you can cope.

Ten of Spades – you will reach the end of your tether.

Jack of Spades – the sign of Sagittarius will be significant and you will have an unexpected visitor.

Queen of Spades – the sign of Leo will be significant and you will hear some gossip.

King of Spades – the sign of Aries will be significant and you will receive an offer of work.

Hearts (Cups in the Tarot deck)

The suit of Hearts, which is associated with the element of water, tells us about things that we have in our hearts and our feelings, and refers to the season of summer.

Ace of Hearts – you will be loved and cherished.

Two of Hearts – you will receive a proposal or a romantic offer.

Cartomancy

Three of Hearts – you will celebrate with friends.
Four of Hearts – someone is thinking of you romantically.
Five of Hearts – you will be filled with sadness or regret.
Six of Hearts – you will receive an apology or have a reunion.
Seven of Hearts – you will choose between two loves.
Eight of Hearts – you will have a change of heart.
Nine of Hearts – your wishes will be granted.
Ten of Hearts – your heart will be filled with joy.
Jack of Hearts – the sign of Pisces will be significant and you will hear of a pregnancy or birth.
Queen of Hearts – the sign of Scorpio will be significant and someone with fair hair will bring good news.
King of Hearts – the sign of Cancer will be significant and an older person will be helpful.

Diamonds (Pentacles or Coins in the Tarot deck)

The suit of Diamonds, which is associated with the element of fire, tells us about our finances and anything to do with how we spend or earn our money, and refers to the season of autumn.

Ace of Diamonds – you will be given the chance to start again.
Two of Diamonds – you will buy new shoes. You will struggle financially.
Three of Diamonds – contracts will be signed and weddings and christenings will be significant.
Four of Diamonds – financial security will come to you.

Five of Diamonds – you will lose money.

Six of Diamonds – you will receive or win money.

Seven of Diamonds – you will find something that you are looking for.

Eight of Diamonds – you will learn something new and work with your hands.

Nine of Diamonds – you will experience a new-found abundance.

Ten of Diamonds – you will study a new subject and have a family reunion.

Jack of Diamonds – the sign of Capricorn will be significant and money will arrive.

Queen of Diamonds – the sign of Aquarius will be significant and an older woman will be helpful.

King of Diamonds – the sign of Gemini will be significant and you will discuss or arrange mortgages, investments or insurances.

Clubs (Swords in the Tarot deck)

The suit of Clubs, which is associated with the element of earth, tells us about the things that we can do or are doing, and refers to the season of winter.

Ace of Clubs – you will feel empowered and be able to achieve things as opposed to merely wishing for them.

Two of Clubs – be patient and do and say nothing.

Three of Clubs – you will shed tears.

Four of Clubs –do not make changes or become involved with another's problems.

Cartomancy

Five of Clubs – gossip and jealousy will upset you.

Six of Clubs – you will move to a new home.

Seven of Clubs – beware of theft and people who cannot be trusted.

Eight of Clubs – you will feel trapped in your present situation.

Nine of Clubs – you will be let down at the last minute.

Ten of Clubs – you will crumble under pressure and feel unable to cope, but things will improve.

Jack of Clubs – the sign of Taurus will be significant and papers will be signed.

Queen of Clubs – the sign of Virgo will be significant and you will experience or witness anger and resentment.

King of Clubs – the sign of Libra will be significant and legal or medical matters will require attention.

Catoptromancy
Crystal Gazing in the Moonlight

This form of divination requires a full moon, a mirror and some warm clothes, especially if it is a chilly night, and, of course, a safe place to work.

Catoptromancy Divination Exercise

Once you have gathered together all the things that you need, place your mirror on the ground or on a suitable surface where it will capture the rays or the reflection of the moon. Make yourself comfortable and sit or stand in front of your mirror and gaze at the reflection of the moon in the mirror. Allow your focus to drift and blur whilst concentrating on any issue that you have on your mind. With practice images may come to you and when you are done note your thoughts or anything of importance that you have felt or seen. Later, when you are at home, you can go over your notes and you can also refer back to them at a later date.

Ceroscopy
Divination Using Wax in Water

This method of divination is messy but interesting. You will need a bowl of water, a lighted candle, your notebook, a pen and a solid surface to work on. Before you attempt to answer a question you should practise dropping the melted wax into the bowl of water and analysing the shapes that form.

Ceroscopy Divination Exercise

Make yourself comfortable and ensure that you will not be disturbed. Prepare all the things that you need – notepad and pen, candle and matches, and, of course, your bowl of water. Focus your attention and allow your mind to drift into a higher state. Recite the following verse:

> *Candle burn and water flow*
> *Show me shapes, that I may know.*

When you are ready take the candle in your right hand, tilt it to one side and allow drops of melted wax to fall into your bowl of water. Try to identify the shapes that form and note them in your notepad. When working with methods of divination that require both hands it is sometimes easier to record your notes on a tape recorder. Later you can copy your impressions into your notepad. When you feel comfortable with this method of divination you can progress to answering single questions.

Cleidomancy
Divination Using a Key

This method of divination can be carried out using a key, a needle or a piece of jewellery and is often referred to as dowsing. You can make your own dowser or pendulum by tying a piece of string to a key, or using a needle suspended from a piece of thread or a ring suspended from a chain. Once you have made your pendulum you can begin to practise using it. Hold your pendulum. Think 'yes' and observe the movement of the object that you are using. It may spin gently in a circular movement or it may swing gently from side to side. Think 'no' and observe the movement or lack of movement. Once you are familiar with this you can try the following exercises.

Cleidomancy Divination Exercise to Find Something That is Lost

Close your eyes and imagine a white light above your head. Allow your thoughts to focus on the lost object and try to think back to the last time that you saw or held the missing item. Hold the pendulum in your right hand, draping the cotton or chain over your index finger so that the ring, key or crystal is suspended about six inches below your hand. Stand in the middle of your room and mentally draw a line down the centre of the floor. Hold the pendulum at arm's length to your right and mentally ask if the item is on this side of the line. Observe the movement. Room by room, then section by section, you can gradually narrow down the location of the missing object. You can also write on pieces of paper various locations or questions, then fold them up, lay them in a line and mentally ask for the answer while holding your pendulum over each one. Keep trying, trust your instincts and this should work for you.

Cleidomancy Divination Exercise One, to Answer a Question

Before you begin, gather together everything that you need – a pen and a piece of paper and your pendulum. Write your question on the piece of paper and then hold your pendulum in your hand. Close your eyes and imagine a white light above your head and allow your thoughts to focus on your question. Now place the pendulum over the question that is written on your piece of paper and watch to see if there is any movement.

Cleidomancy Divination Exercise Two to Answer a Question

For this exercise write the words 'yes' and 'no' on two separate pieces of paper and lay them face down on your work surface. Shuffle the pieces of paper around so that you do not know which one says what. When you are ready, think of your question and then dowse over each piece of paper to find the answer.

Coffee Gazing
Divination Using Coffee Grounds

For me, this is where it all began because when I was small I used to watch my mum fortune telling for neighbours. She insists that it was using cups of coffee but my memory tells me tea. No matter. Either way, coffee gazing is very accurate but only with practice and only if you are totally prepared to trust your instincts. This is a really nice relaxed social method of divining.

Divination Exercise

Make yourself a pot of freshly ground coffee. Do not use a coffee filter. A percolator is fine as long as when the coffee is poured and drank some grains and dust are still left in the cup. It is best to use a shallow, white, fluted cup rather than a mug. If you are reading for someone other than yourself make sure that your guest does not talk about personal issues or discuss the reason why they wish to have a reading.

After the coffee is finished take the guest's cup and look into it. If there are no grains at the bottom of the cup then another cup will be required. If this happens again it could be that you are not meant to read for that person or that they are meant to solve their problem themselves. If there is too much liquid remaining in the cup, slowly pour the excess into a saucer but do not discard it as this too can be read.

Excess liquid is often an indication of tears but these can be tears of joy as well as sadness and the reading will

Coffee Gazing

give you a clue as to which. Undissolved sugar gathered in the cup indicates sweetness, compliments and pleasant times ahead. The symbols that are at the top of the cup are those that are closest in time and those near the bottom are further away in time. Sometimes grounds in the shape of numbers and signs of the Zodiac that are next to symbols will guide you. Study the interpretations at the end of this book and, where you can, memorise them and use them to interpret the shapes you see in the grounds. But do not forget that your intuition will be the most accurate method that you can use.

Crystallomancy
Divination using Crystals

This is a simple form of divination and to use this method it is important to have a good selection of crystals. My interpretations for crystal divination use the more popular, easy to obtain crystals, and even if you only use this form of divination occasionally you will get a great deal of pleasure from the beautiful crystals in your collection.

Preparation and Dedication of Crystals

Make sure that you keep your crystals clean and uncontaminated by negative energies. A simple method for cleaning crystals is to rinse them in spring or even tap water but every now and then I use a mixture of one tablespoonful of cider vinegar water, one tablespoonful of coarse salt and a few pints of warm water. Mix them all together but do not put the crystals into the mixture until the temperature is hand hot. If the water is any hotter than this you could crack some crystals. Leave the crystals to soak for twenty minutes and then rinse in clean running water.

Once you have done this, if you have the time, put them on a windowsill as the moon is rising (waxing) and leave them there until the moon is full. While your crystals are being 'charged' you can busy yourself preparing a mat to work with when you are divining them.

It is best to use a silk cloth. I have one that I use when I am working with my Tarot cards. I bought a plain black napkin and a fabric pen and I drew my favourite spread on my mat. I drew patterns and symbols on it that I wanted to remember. By the time I had finished my project, a week later, I had succeeded in remembering the meanings of the symbols. In addition, I had a cloth that was personalised and that I was very proud of. You can do the same and design it in any way that you choose. Do not worry if you are not good at drawing because you can always buy New Age magazines or books where you will find zodiac symbols that you can trace and then copy onto your mat.

When your mat is ready and your crystals are fully charged the next step is to dedicate your crystals to your purpose. To do so, prepare a work surface and make it as pretty or as simple as you like. Place a candle in a candle holder on your work surface. You could dedicate a green taper candle to the process of finding answers by anointing it with three drops of essential oil of marjoram mixed with 10 ml of almond oil. [After the divination is over let the candle burn down naturally or extinguish with a snuffer but not by blowing out.]

Spread your cloth. Light your candle and spread your charged crystals on the mat. Place both hands, palms down, above the crystals and visualise bright golden white light spreading through your hands from above and covering your crystals and your mat. Say your chosen verse from the list below or use words of your own and spend some time sharing the good energy with your crystals. The same method can be used to cleanse and dedicate a single crystal. When your crystal or crystals are charged and dedicated put them in a small pouch and keep them in the pouch until you are ready to use them.

Verses for Crystal Dedications

Dedication for divination:

> Crystals, pure and filled with light,
> Your purpose true upon this night,
> Let your power shine for me
> In the secrets that you free.

Dedication for recalling dreams:

> A dream I had, but can't recall
> I ask this crystal, which knows all,
> To share with me my sleeping thoughts
> An answer from my dreams is sought.

Dedication for healing:

> Little crystal, power pure
> Bring good health to ***** for sure.
> Your healing power is what I ask
> To help me in my healing task.

Dedication for improved finances:

> Little crystal gleaming bright
> Boost my money, hear my plight
> Better off I wish to be
> So I can be worry free.

Crystallomancy

Dedication for love

> Mutual love, that is good and kind,
> Passionate, faithful and of like mind,
> With crystal power I seek a mate
> I put my trust in you and fate.

Divination Exercise Using Crystals

Now that you are ready to begin, gather all your things ready for use:

> Crystals, in their pouch
> Divining mat
> Candle and holder
> Matches
> A small bowl in which to put spent matches
> A bottle containing 3 drops of essential oil of marjoram and 10 ml of almond oil (with which to anoint your candle if you wish)
> A bowl of water and a flannel to wipe your hands on

Prepare yourself mentally for the task you are about to perform and make sure that your hands are clean. Prepare your work surface with the items listed, make yourself comfortable and, if you are doing this for someone other than yourself, make sure that they are relaxed and comfortable too.

Hold the pouch of crystals in both hands and spend a few quiet moments thinking of your questions and sharing positive energy.

If you are divining for yourself put your left hand into the pouch and draw out one handful of crystals and allow the cystals to fall onto the mat.

If you are divining for someone else pass the pouch of crystals to the person that you are reading for and ask them to hold them, spending a few moments thinking of their questions and sharing positive energy with the crystals. Have the subject put their left hand into the pouch and draw out one handful of crystals and allow them to fall onto the divining mat.

Be aware of the predominance of certain colours The colours will give you clues and the colour chart will help you to understand what you are being told.

- **White** is for purity, cleansing and knowledge.
- **Red** is for passion, excitement and action.
- **Pink** is for love and romance.
- **Orange** is for strength, power and courage.
- **Yellow** is for energy, vitality and motivation.
- **Green** is for healing, growth and fertility.
- **Blue** is for tranquillity and peace.
- **Purple** is for protection, meditation and spirituality
- **Turquoise** is for communication, protection and travel.
- **Black** is for grounding and dispelling negative energies.

Crystallomancy

The numbers formed

Look at the grouping, as you may find that some crystals have separated from the rest and they may be lying in groups of, for example, three or seven. This too may give you greater insight.

- One is the number of leadership, new beginnings, new ideas, and inspiration. One will show exciting new changes ahead.
- Two is the number of tact and diplomacy, balance and harmony. Be prepared for some surprises if the number two is significant.
- Three is the number of pregnancy and nursing or nurturing. Socialising, having good times with friends and joining clubs, societies or organisations will be relevant.
- Four is the number of security, assets and the home. Major changes around the home such as repairs, renovations, and renewals can be expected or visits from older males. Four is a very dependable number.
- Five is the number representing keys that will unlock the answers to your questions or the door to your new home. Five is the number which shows the problem areas in your life, or any conflict that will be experienced. Also linked with the number five are uniforms of any description.
- Six is the number of tenderness, compassion, difficult choices which have to be made, cross roads being

reached, and the eternal triangle. However, where five shows the problems, six is the number that provides the solution.

• Seven is the number of control, and questioning comes in here. Control cannot be obtained without full knowledge of all facts surrounding you. With inner questioning, one can then resume control in one's life.

• Eight is the number of strength, determination and stubbornness. This number will show that you or someone close to you will have to be very stubborn to achieve cherished goals.

• Nine is the number of completion or seeing the light at the end of the tunnel, finding your way after stumbling around in the dark. It represents the completion of difficult tasks.

Once you have examined these things you can then begin to look at the meanings in each separate crystal.

Sample divination

In this reading seven crystals fell.

1 Agate – Difficult obstacles will be overcome.

2 Bloodstone – Legal and business matters will be dealt with and the outcome will be in your favour.

3 Malachite – You will overcome an obstacle that you thought was insurmountable.

4 Labradorite – Be persistent in all your efforts and you will be rewarded.

5 Hematite – You will be offered a helping hand from an unexpected source.

6 Jasper – You will be touched by a sharing experience with someone.

7 Tourmaline Green – You will become more active and your prosperity will increase.

There were seven crystals and so the reading for seven is relevant:

'Seven is the number of control. Control cannot be obtained without full knowledge of all facts surrounding you. With inner questioning, one can then resume control in one's life.'

The crystals fell in two groups:

'Two is the number of tact and diplomacy, balance and harmony. Be prepared for some surprises if the number two is significant.'

There were two crystals in one group: one Malachite and one Agate. Both these crystals indicate that obstacles will be overcome and the significance of the number two indicates that information that you do not have will be revealed and this is what will make the difference.

Five crystals were in the other group: Bloodstone, Labradorite, Hematite, Jasper and Green Tourmaline.

• Bloodstone indicates that legal and business matters will be dealt with and the outcome will be in your favour.

• Labradorite indicates that you should be persistent in

all your efforts and you will be rewarded.
- Hematite indicates that you will be offered a helping hand from an unexpected source.
- Jasper indicates that you will be touched by a sharing experience with someone.
- Tourmaline Green indicates that you will become more active and your prosperity will increase.

'Five is the number representing keys that will unlock the answers to your questions or the door to your new home. Five is the number which shows the problem areas in your life, or any conflict that will be experienced. Also linked with the number five are uniforms of any description.'

I would consider this to be a reading with a good outcome especially as far as business and legal matters are concerned.

Crystal interpretations for divination:

You can use the following interpretations as a guide when divining with crystals:

Agates – Difficult obstacles will be overcome.

Agate Blue Lace – You will receive a letter or telephone call.

Agate Moss – An emotional problem will be solved and you will feel more content with your life.

Amber – You will be blessed with good fortune.

Amethyst – A decision will be made.

Crystallomancy

Aquamarine – Although you may not think so, you will be strong and cope with a difficult situation and all will be well.

Aventurine – You will be given additional responsibilities and financial increase.

Bloodstone – Legal and business matters will be dealt with and the outcome will be in your favour.

Calcite – Old friends will reappear and misunderstandings will be settled.

Carnelian – You will be involved in a passionate affair and the arts will be important.

Celestite – Do not despair, calm will return and your pain will be eased.

Citrine – You will receive an unexpected windfall.

Fluorite – You will be protected from an abusive or aggressive situation or person.

Hematite – You will be offered a helping hand from an unexpected source.

Jade – You will be more organised and this will reflect on other areas of your life and help you to attract what you want.

Jasper – You will be touched by a sharing experience with someone.

Labradorite – Be persistent in all your efforts and you will be rewarded.

Lapis Lazuli – You will enjoy sharing quality time with friends or family members.

Malachite – You will overcome an obstacle that you thought was insurmountable.

Moldavite – An unexpected situation may catch you out but you will deal with whatever comes and do what must be done.

Moonstone – You will hear news of a pregnancy or birth.

Obsidian Black – You will be reluctant to commit to something or to someone's request and you are right to feel this way.

Pearl – Peace will be restored and ther will be a happy outcome to a fretful situation.

Peacock Ore – You will re-evaluate your plans or have a change of heart.

Peridot – You will feel stronger and filled with renewed energy.

Pyrite – You will move to a new location.

Quartz – You will instinctively know what to do next and when to do it.

Rose Quartz – Romance is in the air and you will have a new found happiness.

Ruby – You will be successful in all your endeavours.

Rutilated Quartz – Someone may try to meddle in your affairs but you will politely let them know that their advice or attention is neither required nor helpful.

Sapphire – Partnerships may require some additional attention to improve.

Smoky Quartz – You may have to study a new subject or look more closely at a problem to find the correct solution.

Sodalite – You will receive news that will give a deeper understanding of a person or situation that you are confused about.

Crystallomancy

Tiger-eye – New subjects will be studied and you will be hopeful about a future opening.

Tourmaline – You may feel as though you are stuck in the middle but soon you will make the correct decision and be able to decide where you stand.

Tourmaline Black – An unexpected development will remove you or yours from a difficult situation.

Tourmaline Pink – A new friend will be made or a new romance will begin.

Tourmaline Red – You will be determined to succeed and succeed you shall.

Tourmaline Green – You will become more active and your prosperity will increase.

Turquoise – You will be surprised by conflict among friends or in the workplace. Do not allow yourself to become involved in this.

Cyclomancy
Divination Using a Wheel

I can recall playing with this form of divination as a child and remember getting a coloured card wheel in a 'lucky bag' or perhaps a Christmas cracker. The wheel was divided up into sections like a pie and each section was a different colour and had a different number printed on it.

There was a wooden spindle through the centre and when you twisted it, the wheel spun and finally settled on one part of the edge. The part of the edge that touched the floor indicated the number and colour that related to your question.

Cyclomancy Divination Exercise

You could make your own Cyclomancy fortune telling wheel by cutting a piece of card to the size of a dinner plate. Using a pen, divide the wheel into twelve sections in the form of a pie chart. Colour each section to correspond with the twelve signs of the zodiac and decorate each section with zodiac symbols.

Aries	♈	red
Taurus	♉	red, orange, blue
Gemini	♊	orange, silver, grey
Cancer	♋	silver, white, yellow, orange
Leo	♌	yellow, gold, orange
Virgo	♍	grey, yellow, green
Libra	♎	green, light blue

Cyclomancy

Scorpio	♏	green, blue, dark red
Sagittarius	♐	blue, purple
Capricorn	♑	deep blue, dark green
Aquarius	♒	indigo, pale blue, green
Pisces	♓	violet

Number each section from zero to eleven and then pierce the centre of the wheel with a skewer.

Relax and focus on your wheel and your own thoughts and ask your question in the usual fashion. Spin the wheel and see where it stops. Use the number and colour interpretations listed in this book to help you find your answers. For the number ten read good luck, winning and changes connected to transport or home. For the number eleven, read legal and medical matters and power. The significance of the rest the numbers has been covered under the heading of Arithmomancy.

Dactylomancy
Divination Using a Ring

This method of divination is similar to dowsing, except that a ring is used. The ring is dangled on a piece of cord over words or numbers.

Dactylomancy Divination Exercise

You can try the above method of divining by suspending a ring on a cord or chain and you can obtain your answers just by thinking of the question or by writing things on pieces of paper and then suspending the ring over each piece of paper until the ring spins. Always remember to treat any form of divination (fortune telling) seriously. If you approach it flippantly then it will not work. In any case, you should respect the powers that

Geomancy
Divination Using Random Drawings

Sometimes people refer to this form of divination as ghost writing, spirit writing or automatic writing. (The poet WB Yeats and his wife Georgina were both interested in occult practices – Yeats was a Member of the Order of the Golden Dawn – and they both participated in automatic writing.)

Some people find it really easy to perform and even write books using this method whilst others find it almost impossible to do. The object of the exercise is to allow yourself to drift into a subliminal state while holding a pen and paper and then you wait until your hand begins to spontaneously write.

Geomancy Divination Exercise

First prepare yourself mentally for the task you are about to perform. Make sure your surroundings are neat and tidy and that you will not be disturbed. Have a work surface ready with pen and paper, and perhaps some incense and a candle. Make yourself comfortable and relax.

Place the pen or pencil in your hand over the blank paper and allow yourself to drift into a higher state of awareness. Some people give themselves a fright when they actually start to write things but don't be put off. Just allow the pen or pencil to move and gradually become comfortable with this method. If words are produced, their meaning may be obvious to you or they may need some interpretation. Similarly, if symbols or random drawings are produced that don't initially seem to hold significance for you, you may have to consult the lists of symbols at the end of this book.

After some practice you may find that this is a successful method of divination for you.

Graphology
Divination Using Handwriting

There is a complete science devoted to the study of handwriting. Everything is taken into consideration – the size, style, angle and the shape of the letters, and much more and so there is no space here to do study of the subject justice. I have a simpler method though, using intuition rather than a scientific or psychological approach, that you might like to try.

Graphology Divination Exercise

Ask a friend to bring you a selection of letters or even just the envelopes and begin by practising on these. Hold the letters and scan the handwriting, though not the content, of the letters, allowing your impressions and feelings to guide you rather than attempting a scientific approach. Talk to your friend and describe what you feel when you hold the letters, and the impression you get of the writer's feelings and intentions, and ask your friend to make notes. When you have finished ask your friend whether your conclusions were accurate.

Again, with practice you can perfect this form of divination. If you find you have a particular talent and intuition for 'reading' letters in this way, why not study one of the many books on graphology that are available and expand on your ability.

Gyromancy
Divination by Walking in a Circle

This is simply a much bigger version of Cyclomancy, divination using a wheel. Fans of *Big Brother* in the UK (with long memories) may remember the game that Kate and Tim played in Big Brother 3 when they ran around a brush handle and, in a severe state of dizziness, then were sent running across the room. They had consumed quite a bit of alcohol, and funny though it was, I don't recommend that for this exercise, you'll be dizzy enough. The object of the exercise is to randomly select letters to form words that will give a message or answer a question.

Gyromancy Divination Exercise

Gather together a brush handle, a pack of A4 paper, a marker pen ... and a very good friend who will not think that you have lost your senses! You will need fourteen pieces of A4 paper, each halved in two. Print a letter of the alphabet on each piece of paper and on the last two the words 'yes' and 'no'. Place the papers randomly in a circle on the floor face up. And now the fun begins. Stand in the middle of the circle of papers with your right hand on the top of the brush handle and begin to walk quickly round in a tight circle. When you become dizzy you will begin to stagger about and as you touch a piece of paper your friend should make a note of the letter. With any luck you might just have your question answered – though you'll probably be lauging so much you won't care whether you do or not!

Numerology
Divination Using Numbers

This form of divination has ancient origins, but is also a modern way of interpreting names and dates in terms of vital numbers, all of which are indicative of individual traits. I have been asked in the past to look at why certain individuals have success in their lives while others appear to have nothing but problems. On analysing their numbers I have discovered that those who are successful have positive numbers while those who are beset by problems have negative ones. Numerology is a more in-depth look at arithmomancy and uses all the numbers that are involved in the search.

Have you ever wondered just what makes you tick? Some people will say they are typical of their astrological star sign while others will say that they are nothing like theirs. Why is that so? There is a link between where and when you were born which forms part of your character and decides how you will act in, or react to, given situations in your life, but there is so much more than just the astrological influence at work.

Did you know that the numbers in your date of birth play a very large part in forming your character? In fact, these numbers will motivate and mould you, and their influence will be with you for the rest of your life.

There are also numbers in your name. Alan, for example, is a one and this is the number of leadership. Anyone whose name adds up to one should never be afraid to follow his or her dreams. They will also have moments of pure genius but it is up to them whether or not they pursue these insights. Unlike your birth number, your name number is not constant. It can change if, for example, you have a nickname. If Alan is sometimes called Al he then becomes a four, and the influences of this number are different. As a four he will be more concerned with stability and security, and will not be easily unsettled in a crisis. He is so dependable as a four that often friends or family will go to him for advice or support.

It is important also to look at surnames because these too influence our lives. When a woman takes a man's name in marriage she drops her surname and its number and adopts his surname and his number. Sometimes this complements the numbers and attributes that she already has, although on other occasions it can create conflict or negative influences. So, if you've just got married and feel out of kilter, don't immediately jump to the conclusion that all is not well, it might just be your numbers. There is a solution though – just by changing how you spell your name you can make a difference. For example, Anne adds up to eight whereas Ann adds up to two. It's only when we know and understand the meaning of numbers and how they influence our lives that we can begin to use them to our advantage.

Two of my clients are celebrities who were out of work and not achieving their potential. They felt that they were not being recognised for their talents. After an initial consultation I was able to discover that they each had influences in their names that were not significant to success in their chosen fields. With a few changes to the spelling of their names they have both gone on to have successful careers.

Most people will have a lucky number, or a number that has some special significance to them. So if you are going to try the next exercise, jot down on a piece of paper the number or numbers that you feel are important to you.

Numerology Divination Exercise – Character Analysis

Before you begin you must find the numbers that are significant to you. Start off by using the number and letter chart below to find the numbers that are relevant in your date of birth and your name.

Birth Number

This is the number that motivates your life. This is obtained by adding the numbers in your date of birth.

For example, Dave Reynolds' date of birth is
22.12.1949
$(2 + 2 + 1 + 2 + 1 + 9 + 4 + 9) = 30$
$(3 + 0) = 3$

Birth number $= 3$

Your birth number is the number that motivates and moulds you throughout your life and, unlike your name number, no changes can be made here.

Name Number

The next step is to find your name numbers. Use the following chart to change the letters of your name to their numerical value. Most people consider this their lucky number.

1	2	3	4	5	6	7	8	9
A	B	C	D	E	F	G	H	I
J	K	L	M	N	O	P	Q	R
S	T	U	V	W	X	Y	Z	

First Name Number

Write your first name and its associated numbers, and add the numbers together as you did for your birth number.

For example:

D   A   V   E
4   1   4   5 = 14
1 + 4
First name number = 5

Here the major influence in the first name Dave is five. Include any other name that you have if it is used in your daily life. For example, your first names may be Sarah and Jane, and you are addressed as Sarah Jane. My other first name is Elizabeth but it is a name that is never used so I do not consider it when working with numerology.

Your first name displays the character that you show to your friends, those people who address you by no other name than your first name.

Now find the vowels in your first name, enter them in the grid below and add them together until you again have a single digit.

Vowel Number

For example:

D	A	V	E
	1		5 = 6

The vowels in your first name will show your inner personality. This is the side of your character or nature that you keep to yourself.

Consonant Number

Now find the consonants in your first name, enter them below and add them together until you again have a single digit.

For example:

D	A	V	E
4		4	= 8

The consonants in your first name will show the side of your nature that you allow others to see, your outer personality.

Surname Number

Now repeat this exercise with your surname.

R	E	Y	N	O	L	D	S
9	5	7	5	6	3	4	1

$9 + 5 + 7 + 5 + 6 + 3 + 4 + 1 = 40$

$4 + 0 = 4$

Whole Name Number

Now add together your first name number and your surname number only.

Dave Reynolds' first name number is 5 and his srurname number is 4, therefore his whole name number is 9.

The whole name number displays the character that you show to associates or in situations where you are required to sign your name.

Destiny Number

The next step is to find your destiny number. Your destiny number is a combination of your name and birth numbers and, as with your name number, changes can occur here through marriage, divorce or choice.

For example:
Birth number: 3
Whole name number: 9

Add the two together until you have a single digit:

$3 + 9 = 12$

$1 + 2 = 3$

Dave Reynolds' destiny number is 3.

Prediction Number

This will show the general indications for any month of any year and must be recalculated each year as your numbers will change from year to year. To discover your monthly number you must first take your destiny number and then add the value of the month and year in question. Each month has its own value and the following table will help you with your calculations.

Jan = 1	Feb = 2	Mar = 3
Apr = 4	May = 5	June = 6
July = 7	Aug = 8	Sep = 9
Oct = 1	Nov = 2	Dec = 3

Example:

To calculate the month of October 2006 for Dave Reynolds the following formula is used:

His destiny number = 3

October = 1

$2006 (2 + 0 + 0 + 6) = 8$

This new total is the prediction number =

$3 + 1 + 8 = 12$

$1 + 2 = 3$

You can expand on this by adding the entire date, For example, to use the date 25/04/2004 the numbers that you would add together would be:

For the day = 2 + 5 = 7
For the month = 4
For the year 2004 = (2+0 + 0 + 4) = 6
Total = 7 + 4 + 6 = 15 = 1 + 5 = 6
Then Dave would add his destiny number to the number six.
6 + 3 = 9

To recap:

Dave's first name number	5
Dave's inner personality	6
Dave's outer personality	8
Dave's full name	9
Dave's birth number	3
Dave's destiny number	3

Missing numbers

Pay close attention to the numbers that do not appear in your profile since you can learn a lot about your character here too. If you choose, you can add these numbers into your name by adding an initial (number) in between your first name and surnames.

Definition of Name Numbers

One: This is the first number and people who have the

number one as their name number tend to be leaders. They like to be first at everything – first in the queue, first to know something and, of course, first to do things. These people are, or appear to be, generally impulsive and often have moments of sheer brilliance. They are more likely to be leaders than followers, they are generally very popular socially and professionally. They have the courage of their convictions and are not afraid to speak their minds. Negative aspects, however, may make them appear to be pushy, forceful, eccentric, egotistical, domineering and sometimes paranoid or self-conscious. If you have this number as your name number, recognise your positive traits and work with them, and do your best to avoid the negative aspects of this influence.

Two: This is the number of balance and harmony, truth and beauty. People who have this name number are generally very deep, and friends and family members may feel as though they never really know what they are thinking. This person will mostly be respected and admired because they make good friends or companions and are helpful in difficult situations without becoming too involved. They are good judges of character and when they have made up their mind about something they are difficult to shift. They prefer to follow rather than lead but they are very capable of leading without any difficulty. Negative aspects that these individuals have are being secretive and picky, as well as sometimes narrow-minded and biased.

Three: People whose name corresponds to this number tend to be friendly and outgoing yet sympathetic and charitable. They will be self-sacrificing and would do without to help another. Very often these individuals trust their instincts. Although they are ambitious, they value their security and are unlikely to make rash decisions. They will have good friends and make entertaining and interesting company. Capable of overcoming obstacles, they will achieve their ambitions. A negative trait is beingover-indulgent and excessive on the social scene.

Four: This is a very dependable name number and people whose name corresponds to four can be relied upon in a crisis and make true and loyal friends. They value and respect their homes, and property matters will concern them to the extent that a second home will be desired and probably obtained. They like to be active and involved in a variety of things and will have many interesting experiences. On the negative side, they can fall to pieces if they have a crisis of their own to deal with and become despondent if others think that they can cope instead of offering a helping hand. They can also be a little boring, valuing their security to the extreme.

Five: People whose name corresponds to this number are likely to be extremely curious and will often answer a question with another question. For example, if you say: 'Why did that happen?' they are likely to say: ' Why do you ask?' They change their friends as often as they change their shoes and absolutely must have variety in their life to survive. On the negative side, they can be ruthless and nosey and, at worst, enjoy spreading gossip.

Six: People whose name corresponds to this number will always find it hard to make decisions or choices. Although when asked a favour they will say 'yes', they will often avoid carrying out the favour, believing it is easier to say 'yes' and let someone down rather than say 'no' in the first place. They are, however, among the kindest and most charitable people. On the negative side they cannot be depended upon and are often infuriating when it comes to decision-making.

Seven: This is the number that is associated with control, and people whose name corresponds to this figure will want to do things their own way in spite of any advice or guidance that they may be offered. On the surface they may appear to be reckless and have a tendency to make rash decisions, when in fact they have probably thought long and hard before making their choice and simply have not discussed this with anyone. They tend to be studious and intellectual, and often have an amazing collection of books on a variety of spiritual and unusual subjects. On the negative side, they can be domineering and forceful, and expect to have everything their own way.

Eight: This is the number of strength and determination, and people whose number corresponds to the number eight will have strong personalities. They are very honest, balanced and hard working, and will persevere with a problem or task when others have long since given up. They appear to be placid and even-tempered but when pushed they have a tendency to erupt like a volcano.

Nine: This is the number of completion and blesses the bearer with the ability to complete tasks that others cannot cope with. Friendly and charming, individuals whose number corresponds to nine often appear rather eccentric, and are changeable like the weather. They have vivid imaginations and are capable of making up stories that will entertain and amuse, but you only discover this when you really get to know them as initially they can appear refined and stand-offish.

Eleven and twenty-two are power numbers that hold special significance and so should be analysed without being reduced like the others.

Eleven: Anyone who corresponds to this name number will be a strong, powerful individual who will possess the courage to take on any challenge and also the persistence to see it through to the end. They thirst for adventure and quickly become bored with the more mundane aspects of life. On the negative side, they are restless and intolerant of others who are not as smart as they are.

Twenty-Two: People whose name corresponds to this number will always feel as though they are on the edge of something great – but they usually do not have the courage to take the next step. They tend to act younger than their years and sometimes blame others or outside circumstances for their lack of success. People with this name number have to work very, very hard to achieve.

Definition of Birth and Destiny Numbers

One: You will lead rather than follow and reach the top of any career that you choose. You will make your own choices and if someone else has already done something you will know that you can too. If no one has achieved a particular thing then you will decide that you can be the first. The sign of Capricorn will be prominent in your life.

Two: Although your life will be interesting and successful you could do better if you chose to. Law, medicine and journalism may interest you. With the ability to listen to both sides of an argument and find a happy medium you would make an excellent arbitrator. The sign of Aquarius will be prominent in your life.

Three: You will have many friends and be liked and admired by them all. The caring professions will attract you because you will enjoy looking after the needs of others less fortunate than yourself. Children, family, pets and horticulture will be significant and important to you. The signs of Pisces and Scorpio will be prominent in your life.

Four: Your life will be successful because of the effort you put into it and nothing will hold you back or stand in your way. Property and all things connected to property will attract you, and friends will come to recognise your reliability to do what you say and say what you mean. The sign of Aries will be prominent in your life.

Five: You will have a varied and interesting life because you will do everything in your power to make it so. Engineering, investigative journalism, the police force, the military and education will be of some interest or significance. The sign of Taurus will be prominent in your life.

Six: Do not be afraid to take a few chances or make changes in your life, otherwise when you are older you will find yourself saying 'I remember the chances I missed,' or 'I wish I could do it all over again,' and 'I would do this or that.' If you take the odd chance you can be successful. The sign of Gemini will be prominent in your life.

Seven: Success, success, success. You are off to a good start and from there you will make things happen. However, you will have to work hard for it though. Sometimes you may feel frustrated at other's inadequacies but you will shine and outshine those who compete with you. The sign of Cancer will be prominent in your life.

Eight: You will be hard-working, eager to succeed and diligent in your efforts. Financially, you may not be very good at looking after your money. 'Save' is the key word that you should remember and then you can help to overcome or even avoid this negative tendency. The sign of Leo will be prominent in your life.

Nine: You will enjoy a variety of experiences and, although this will make you an interesting individual, you may find that you come across as a 'know it all'. Only a nine could cram so much into one life and this is because you find it hard to stick to one thing. On the positive side you will find that this variety of experiences gives you the ability to be able to turn your hand to almost anything and you will be a great help in an emergency because of your ability to know what to do next. Well, you will have seen it all before! The sign of Virgo will be prominent in your life.

Eleven: If you are involved in group activities you will be the one to take control because yours is a power number. The only time that this may not be true is when another person in the same group also has the number eleven in their profile. Then the power struggle will begin and others will watch in amazement. You will make your mind up about situations or people very quickly and if you do not like what you see or hear you will turn and walk away without a backward glance. You will be successful in your life because you will grab opportunities and make the most of them. If they do not suit you later, you will drop them. The sign of Libra will be prominent in your life.

Twenty-Two: You will be responsible for creating your own problems and will most certainly be your own worst enemy. Knowing this, you can change it and be observant of your attitude and actions. You can be easily led or manipulated and should be more cautious of the company that you keep and the people that you trust. Success can be yours but only if you can learn from your mistakes and overcome a tendency to act immaturely and not face up to your responsibilities. The sign of Sagittarius will be prominent in your life.

Prediction Numbers

When you are trying to find out what a particular day will hold for you, calculate the date and your destiny number together as you have been shown in the previous pages. Keep adding up the numbers until you have a single digit and then look at the list below to see if you are forecast a good or not-so-good day.

Numerology

One: New business and career opportunities will come during this time and you will form new friendships. This is an important and lucky time and you can do or achieve almost anything that your heart desires.

Two: Patience will be required as things will not happen as quickly as you would like. There is likely to be a house move in the near future and overseas travel will be important. Old friends will return and a few surprises will catch you out.

Three: Accomplishment, recognition and the realisation of ambitions are forecast. Marriage or new business partnerships are highlighted. Make the most of this vibration as everything is possible. News of a pregnancy or a birth will be significant.

Four: Concentrate on the home, property and business matters and do not burn the candle at both ends. Your focus should be on your finances, your security and your stability. People who are older than you will be important.

Five: Change, change, change. Contracts and documents will be important. Complete transformations are possible. This is a good time to take chances, but only if you are aware of all the facts and figures.

Six: Renewing old friendships and settling differences is

possible now. A happy home life and success in relationships is in store. Your soulmate will be very significant at this time.

Seven: In business this is a prosperous time, but care should be exercised when making large purchases. You are warned not to work too hard. Expect the unexpected.

Eight: You will now begin to see the results of efforts that you have made in the past, even though it feels as though it has been a long time coming. This is a good time to invest in property.

Nine: Completion of projects is forecast here and the need to take a little time to yourself. Avoid impulsive actions and think carefully before embarking on new directions.

Eleven: At this time you will be able to realise your ambitions and overcome any obstacles that have been standing in your way. Expect good news concerning legal medical or business matters.

Twenty-Two: Stay close to home, do not make any changes and be careful whom you trust. Reschedule any important meetings to a day that corresponds to a better number. Youngsters may cause you problems too.

Numerology

Further Clues

1	Beginnings	29	Permanence
2	Surprises	30	Contentment
3	Pregnancy	31	Confusion
4	Property	32	News
5	Keys	33	Accomplishment
6	Lovers	34	Travel
7	Arrivals	35	Burdens
8	Persistence	36	Despair
9	Reunions	37	Pisces
10	Luck	38	Romance
11	Justice	39	Scorpio
12	Change	40	Cancer
13	Peace	41	Love
14	Caution	42	Marriage
15	Fear	43	Celebration
16	Despair	44	Depression
17	Fame	45	Sadness
18	Betrayal	46	Reunion
19	Brightness	47	Choices
20	Interviews	48	Re-evaluation
21	Endings	49	Accomplishment
22	Caution	50	Bliss
23	Sagittarius	51	Taurus
24	Abuse	52	The unexpected
25	Leo	53	Virgo
26	Aries	54	Libra
27	Impregnation	55	Division
28	Temporariness	56	Tolerance
		57	Grief

58 Caution
59 Conflict
60 Movement
61 Theft
62 Prison
63 Disappointment
64 Exhaustion
65 Capricorn
66 Chance
67 Aquarius
68 Gemini
69 Opportunity
70 Struggle
71 Celebration
72 Security
73 Poverty
74 Windfall
75 Find
76 Receptions
77 Abundance
78 Study
79 Nostalgia

80 Perseverance
81 Conclusions
82 Surprises
83 Success
84 Change
85 Endings
86 Decisions
87 Fear
88 Crisis
89 Accomplishment
90 Answers
91 Excitement
92 Triumph
93 Transformation
94 Loss
95 Self-control
96 Dread
97 Disaster
98 Reputation
99 Misery
100 Inevitability

Psychometry
Divination Using Touch

Some time ago I was having a coffee and a chat with a biker friend of mine. Del hadn't a clue about tarot, divination, runes or any of the subjects that I love. If you had asked him about his higher self he would have looked at you with an expression of panic and confusion. Anyway, we were sitting having a chat and he asked me if I could tell him anything about himself. Here we go again, I thought, but I began by looking at his name and date of birth and the number that made up his profile. He was so amazed that he asked me if I would read his tarot cards. I did that too and again he was stunned by all the things that I knew about him.

By this time I was getting pretty fed up and tired answering all his questions but he was on a roll. 'Tell me more, tell me more,' he said.

'Right, this is the last thing that I am going to do for you; get me something that you have had for a long time.'

He jumped up from his chair and dashed about looking for something for me to hold. Forgetting that Del knew nothing about divination, I thought to myself, 'Why doesn't he just give me his ring or his watch?'

'Here, try these,' he said, coming back into the room with his slippers. I laughed so much the tears were running down my face. Of course, he didn't know what I was laughing at and I was laughing too much to tell him. But it worked. I actually did read his slippers. That is what psychometry is all about, reading what you feel using the power of touch.

Psychometry Divination Exercise

Invite a few of your friends around one evening for a practice session on psychometry and tell them to bring pieces of jewellery (not slippers!). Have them put these items into a dish. Put a piece of your jewellery into the dish too. When everyone is comfortable and relaxed take turns choosing a piece of jewellery from the dish and begin to discern what you see and feel. No one should guide you in any way and you might find that you instinctively know who the piece belongs to. Say everything that you see or feel and ask someone to take notes. When you are finished, someone else can take a turn. If this is practised regularly you can achieve some amazing results.

Runes
Divination Using an Ancient Wisdom

Everyone, all over the world, from every kind of walk of life, is familiar with the use of symbols or signs in their communication. We have them on our roads telling us to slow down, speed up or stop. Supermarkets, oil companies, political parties, the Church and the medical profession, to name just a few, all use symbols to identify their organisations and the elements within them. Some symbols are modern, designed by graphic designers and artists in marketing companies, but some are drawn from history and tradition. Here we are going to look at some symbols that come from ancient Nordic culture: the Runes.

Of all the esoteric disciplines that are used today, for me, the runes have proved themselves time and again to be among the most accurate of them all.

The Scottish National Party uses a runic symbol called Othel or Othillo, which can be interpreted to stand for home, family and integrity. When we cross our fingers to make a wish, we are making another symbol called *Gefu*, which represents harmony and togetherness.

I was fascinated when I first became acquainted with runes and I wondered how they could help me in my life. I put them in an onyx box and kept them beside my bed. Each night before I went to sleep I would draw one rune, asking as I did so, 'What have I experienced today?' It was not long before I realised how accurate they were. Later, I would draw one in the morning, asking what the day would have in store for me. I managed to take advantage of opportunities that were shown to me and to avoid some pitfalls too.

When you are using the runes for guidance, it is very important to think of one question only. Also runes cannot answer an 'either-way' question. You can ask 'What will be the result if I do this?' but you cannot ask, 'Is it better to do this or that?' When you have prepared a single question in your mind, draw a rune from the box or bag where you keep them. You can draw again for other questions, but no more than three times in any day.

There are twenty-five runic symbols and each one represents a letter of the Germanic alphabet. Each rune tells a historical story to help us to understand or deal with issues in our lives. Some runes, no matter which way they fall, look exactly the same.

An x, for example, looks the same both ways while others in the upside down position give a more negative interpretation. I have listed the runes below in alphabetical order with a brief description so that you can easily refer to them. If you would like to know more see my *Book of the Runes*.

Ansur or *Ansuz* for communication

Runes

Beork or *Berkana* for rebirth, new beginnings and fertility

Dagaz or *Daeg* for hope and promise

Eoh for reliability and travel

Eolh for friendship and protection

Fehu for wealth, property, power and status

Gefu or *Geofu* for partnerships, marriages and engagements

Hagall or *Hagalaz* for projects or situations

Ing or *Inguz* for fertility

Runes

Isa or Is represents a standstill

Jara or Ger represents rewards for your efforts

Ken or *Kano* for openings and invitations

Lagu for water related topics and the feminine element

Mann or *Mannaz* for true
sharing friendship

Neid or *Nauthiz* for restrictions
or problem areas

Othel or *Othillo* for the home,
family and integrity

Peorth or *Perth* for secrets and
hidden information

Runes

 Rado or *Rad* for travel and transport

 Sigel for victory.

 Thorn or *Thurizas* for cautious action

 Tir or *Teiwaz* for winning

Uruz for overcoming
challenges

Wunjo or *Wynn* for joy

the
blank
rune

Wyrd for the inevitable

Yr for continuous effort

Tarot
Divination Using Tarot Cards
(See also CARTOMANCY)

Prepare yourself and your cards and either ask your question or ask for guidance. Then, when you feel ready, draw one card from the pack. You can either choose the top card or you can fan your cards in front of you and choose the card that feels right to you.

If you don't understand what you are being told or if you draw a court card that relates to the astrological sign of someone you know, you can draw an additional card.

The Three-Card Spread

Prepare yourself as before and this time draw three cards. You can ask to be given guidance for past, present, and future or for a particular issue. You are in control here and you will be given any guidance that is available, providing you ask in the first place. As with the earlier spread you can draw an additional card or cards if necessary.

Tarot Interpretations
The Major Arcana

0 The Fool

The Fool in a reading shows that you are coming to the end of a cycle and that a new one of some importance is about to begin. The fool can be looked upon as the bridge to be crossed.

1 The Magician

This is an exciting card. Having completed a cycle of life's experiences, you are about to begin another. You are being given the chance to do it all again and this time you can do it without mistakes, providing you remember those made in the past and the lessons that have been learned from them.

2 The High Priestess

The High Priestess is known as The Keeper of Secrets and The Mistress of Destiny. She contains all the wisdom and knowledge of times gone by and times to come. Patience will be required during this waiting time. Papers, certificates and documents will be important. There will be surprises, renewals and reunions. Higher education is also indicated.

3 The Empress

The Empress is an indication of pregnancy, and can also show someone who is involved in a caring profession, such as maternity care, childcare, care of the elderly, social work or teaching.

4 The Emperor

The Emperor shows major changes around the structure of your life. This can mean a change of job, a change of residence or someone moving into the home. Security and stability are shown by the appearance of this card.

Tarot

5 The High Priest

Keys, promotion, advancement and opportunities are associated with this card. Buildings of historical or architectural importance and uniforms can be significant.

6 The Lovers

Your soulmate is with you or will appear. Choices will have to be made here, and which direction, which job, which partner can be some of the questions asked.

7 The Chariot

Since the chariot is a mode of transport, this card can be telling you about changes around your vehicle. Driving lessons and tests can be significant here. This is also a card which speaks of new directions being pursued and of unexpected arrivals.

8 Strength

The key words are strength, determination, and persistence. You are being told to hang in there. Although you may feel things are not going your way, you will soon reach a conclusion or find a solution.

9 The Hermit

Someone or something will enter your life bringing solutions to problems, an end to loneliness and light at the end of the tunnel. This card can also indicate a child being born.

10 The Wheel

This card indicates gatherings and getting together with friends. Since the wheel links to movement and travel, you can be looking at changes regarding your vehicle. New tyres, tax discs and driving tests can be significant here.

11 Justice

Any official, legal or medical matters will be resolved with a good result. Something that went wrong in the past will be righted on your behalf.

12 The Hanged Man

Suspended animation or being stuck in a rut is exactly how you will be feeling when The Hanged Man appears in a reading. This will change overnight and a very active period will begin.

13 Death

A period of turbulence and sadness is coming to an end and will be replaced by security and stability.

14 Temperance

Go with the flow for the time being and try to exercise moderation in everything that you do. There are indications within this card that you or someone close to you has a dependency problem.

15 The Devil
Fear is the key here. You may be afraid to make changes in your life or experience panic attacks. Opportunities will be missed if this fear is not overcome.

16 The Tower
The Tower can be your worst nightmare. It can range from losing your purse to losing everything that you have. It can be over in a second or it can go on for a long time. Some people call it a run of bad luck. This card denotes misfortune, but before you panic, look to the other cards that accompany it in a spread to make your interpretation.

17 The Star
This is a beautiful card because it speaks of hopes being fulfilled and dreams being realised. Brightness and recognition are indicated as well as opportunities and chances that will be presented to you.

18 The Moon
Depression, anxiety, feeling stabbed in the back and not knowing who to trust are shown with this card.

19 The Sun
This is such a happy card after the previous one. It bestows brightness, joy, vitality and many other positive qualities. This card is especially potent when it appears after or covering a difficult one.

20 Judgement

When Judgement comes into a spread, it is referring to some kind of confrontation. You will either instigate this or be the recipient of it. If your conscience is clear then you have nothing to worry about.

21 The World

The World card indicates that a cycle is being completed and you are being advised that you are going to be given a chance to start again. The World is an indication that everything is achievable and distance is no object. Patience will be required.

The Minor Arcana
The Suit of Wands

Wands are connected to Air and so remember that when you see them in a spread you are mainly looking at thoughts and ideas. That is to say, how you think or will think. Wands are symbolic of artistic or creative projects, such as writing, drawing or painting, but they can also show mundane, ordinary chores or tasks.

The Ace of Wands

This card brings excitement, enthusiasm and motivation, symbolising a new lease of life.

The Two of Wands

This card brings surprising changes. It symbolises temporary conditions such as planning a short break.

Tarot

The Three of Wands
This card denotes the making of plans and looking forward to the future.

The Four of Wands
This card indicates peace of mind and contentment in and around the area that this card occupies. Refer to the cards surrounding this one too.

The Five of Wands
This card indicates conflict and confusion, too many obstacles or problems in your way.

The Six of Wands
This card indicates that you will get a good result regarding something. You will hear good news, or feel a sense of victory.

The Seven of Wands
This card indicates that you should stick to your principles and not back down.

The Eight of Wands
This card indicates that packing and unpacking suitcases will be important.

The Nine Wands
This card indicates that problems and responsibilities will overwhelm you.

The Ten of Wands
You will feel as though you have reached the end of your tether. You have, as this is the end of the present period of difficulties.

The Knight of Wands
This card indicates emotional, verbal or physical abuse. Road rage or minor road accidents might also be represented. If this appears with the tower in the same house or a connected house, the situation will be major and care should be used when explaining this.

NEVER leave a querent (person addressing the cards with a question) with fear.

The Page of Wands, Sagittarius
This card indicates that you will recieve long-distance letters, telephone calls, invitations and visitors.

The Queen of Wands, Leo
This card means that you will hear a piece of news or information to your advantage.

The King of Wands, Aries
This card suggests that a job offer or business opportunity will be given.

The Suit of Cups

The first thing to remember when you are looking at Cups is that they are linked to water which is connected to our emotions. When Cups appear in a reading they are referring to how you feel or will feel about things. Bear in mind the significance of the number of the card as this will help your interpretation.

The Ace of Cups
This card symbolises perfect truth, love and harmony.

The Two of Cups
This card indicates proposals, promises or contracts.

The Three of Cups
This card denotes celebrations, gatherings and heartfelt joy.

The Four of Cups
This card indicates that someone is thinking of making you an offer.

The Five of Cups
This card expresses that the querent is looking back with sadness and regret, wishing things could be as they were.

The Six of Cups
This card symbolises apologies and memories from the past returning.

The Seven of Cups
This card warns that you should choose carefully and not sell yourself short.

The Eight of Cups
This card symbolises the re-evaluation of your life and the making of changes.

The Nine of Cups
This card indicates that, whatever they are, your wishes will be granted.

The Ten of Cups
This card indicates that things will turn out much better than you expect.

The Knight of Cups
This card indicates that friendship, romance, and love that are linked to your past, are about to come back into your life.

The Page of Cups, Pisces
This card indicates that a small gift will be offered and you will hear of a pregnancy.

The Queen of Cups, Scorpio
This card indicates that contentment and happiness is promised.

The King of Cups, Cancer
This card symbolises a generous offer, a kindred spirit or someone or something that will be supportive.

Tarot

The Suit of Swords

Swords are all about actions and words. Although some of the sword cards bring good influences, most bring problems and have to be handled carefully. Look to the other cards in the spread for guidance.

The Ace of Swords
This card symbolises decisive action, clean breaks, fresh starts and purpose and direction.

The Two of Swords
This card indictes the need to tolerate situations that cannot be influenced.

The Three of Swords
This card symbolises grief and heartache.

The Four of Swords
This is a warning: do not get involved in other people's problems or you will be blamed for causing them.

The Five of Swords
Conflict, accusations, arguments and hassle. You are caught in the middle of other people's problems and are being blamed.

The Six of Swords
With the appearance of this card, a house or job move is indicated.

The Seven of Swords
This card indicates that a thief is around, be careful of personal security.

The Eight of Swords
This card could indicate that you feel trapped or restricted. Its symbolism may be more literal – you may hear of someone who has been given a jail sentence.

The Nine of Swords
This card indicates that you feel as though you just can't take any more, but another problem will be revealed.

The Ten of Swords
This card indicates that you feel as though you've reached the end of your tether. This is the last straw but a fresh start will come soon.

The Knight of Swords
This card symbolises a sudden change in circumstances will sweep you off your feet.

The Page of Swords, Taurus
This card could indicate an official demand for money, or official documents that require further action.

The Queen of Swords, Virgo
This card symbolises anger, resentment and bitterness – either being felt, expressed or heard of.

Tarot

The King of Swords, Libra
This card indicates the involvement of a lawyer, doctor, dentist or professional person acting on your or another person's behalf.

The Suit of Pentacles

Pentacles are about money, security, work, assets and opportunities.

The Ace of Pentacles
This card indicates a chance to start again, a golden opportunity.

The Two of Pentacles
This is a card of mixed metaphors: you are walking a tightrope, trying to make ends meet and spreading yourself too thin. In short, your time, money and patience are being stretched.

The Three of Pentacles
This card symbolises the signing of contracts and/or the receiving of a sum of money.

The Four of Pentacles
This card symbolises financial security and stability.

The Five of Pentacles
This card symbolises deprivation, loss of security and fear of the future.

The Six of Pentacles
This card symbolises a windfall, unexpected financial gains.

The Seven of Pentacles
This card indicates that financial help will come from an unexpected source.

The Eight of Pentacles
This card denotes working for yourself or being responsible for how much you can earn through commissions or bonuses. It could indicate that you will soon be earning more money or learning new manual skills.

The Nine of Pentacles
This card symbolises abundance and security.

The Ten of Pentacles
This card indicates the achievement of new academic skills because of, or leading to, new opportunities.

The Knight of Pentacles
This card symbolises an offer which at first does not look very important, although it will develop into something more significant.

The Page of Pentacles, Capricorn
This card indicates that you will receive a valuable gift,

Tarot

money or a cheque.

The Queen of Pentacles, Aquarius
This card symbolises achieving or receiving financial security.

The King of Pentacles, Gemini
This card indicates that bank managers, accountants, financial advisers or influencial people will be supportive.

Tasseography
Divination using tea leaves (see coffee gazing)

Zodiac
Divining the future through the positions of the planets

The twelve signs of the Zodiac are traditionally subdivided into a number of groups.

Triplicities or Elements

Fire

Aries, Leo and Sagittarius are the fire triplicity. Subjects of this element are represented by a keenness and enthusiasm in all their ventures – a fire for life – but also a potential for a certain impatience and selfishness.

Earth

Taurus, Virgo and Capricorn are the earth triplicity. This element is summed up by the phrase 'down to earth'. Earth signs are practical and reliable but can be considered dull by the more lively signs.

Air

Gemini, Libra and Aquarius form the air triplicity. They are full of ideas and exciting ventures, but as the symbolism suggests, these might be 'up in the air' as their practical or cautious side is sometimes lacking.

Water

Cancer, Scorpio and Pisces form the water triplicity which is characterised by emotion, intuition and a desire to be protective of others. They have the potential to let their strong emotions overrule their common sense sometimes.

Quadruplicities or Qualities

Cardinal signs

Aries, Libra, Cancer and Capricorn are of cardinla quadruplicity. This means that peolple with this sign dominant in their chart are outgoing and tend to lead.

Fixed signs

Taurus, Scorpio, Leo and Aquarius are of fixed quadruplicity. These signs show a desire to remain stable, maintain normality, and show a resistance to change.

Mutable signs

Gemini, Sagittarius, Virgo and Pisces all have the ability to accept and welcome change. They adapt to fit environments.

Positive and Negative, Masculine and Feminine

Positive, Masculine

Aries, Gemini, Leo, Libra, Sagittarius and Aquarius have more of a tendency towards the qualities of being self-expressive and extrovert.

Negative, Feminine

Taurus, Cancer, Virgo, Scorpio, Capricorn and Pisces have more of tendency towards the qualities of being receptive and introvert.

Polarity

On a circular representation of the signs the following signs are opposite each other. However, this does not mean they are complete opposites. In fact they have very compatible qualities and complement each other.

Aries and Libra   Cancer and Capricorn
Taurus and Scorpio   Leo and Aquarius
Gemini and Sagittarius   Virgo and Pisces

Planets

Each sign has a ruling planet, each planet has a sign in which it works well (exaltation), a sign in which it is debilitated (detrimental), and a sign in which it is weak (fall). These are shown below:

Planet		Ruling	Exalted	Detrimental	Fall
Sun	☉	Leo	Aries	Aquarius	Libra
Moon	☽	Cancer	Taurus	Capricorn	Scorpio
Mercury	☿	Gemini and Virgo	Virgo	Sagittarius	Pisces
Venus	♀	Taurus and Libra	Pisces	Aries	Virgo
Mars	♂	Aries	Capricorn	Libra	Cancer
Jupiter	♃	Sagittarius	Cancer	Gemini	Capricorn
Saturn	♄	Capricorn	Libra	Cancer	Aries
Uranus	♅ ♁	Aquarius	Scorpio	Leo	Taurus
Neptune	♆	Pisces	Leo	Virgo	Aquarius
Pluto	♇ ♀	Scorpio	Virgo	Taurus	Pisces

The Sun Signs

Aries ♈
The First Sign of the Zodiac: 21 March–20 April

Born under the Fire sign of Aries, a cardinal sign that is ruled by Mars, your fortunate gemstones are amethyst, diamond, bloodstone and opal. The colour red and the numbers six and seven are important to you and your best day of the week is Tuesday. Your best choices of occupation are in the fields of security, law and the military, and you can be very successful in running your own business. Your most fortunate location to live or work in is a large city. You are most compatible with the signs Aries, Gemini, Libra, Leo, Sagittarius and Aquarius, but you do not favour the signs of Taurus, Cancer, Scorpio, Capricorn, Virgo and Pisces.

You have a dynamic personality and can be very intense, and you need plenty of fresh air, sunshine and good food to support your drive. Your sign governs the head and face and these are the areas where you will be most susceptible to ailments. Look after your eyes, teeth and gums, and avoid head colds and throat infections. One of the advantages that you have is that when stricken, you recover well. In affairs of the heart you can be extremely sensitive but can be prone to jealousy and this is something that you should avoid.

Your earning capacity is good however you are inclined to be a generous spender and you prefer to have the very best rather than what you can afford.

As a friend you are very loyal but, when crossed, you can be unforgiving and tend to hold a grudge. You should try to be more patient with yourself and others.

The Aries child will require careful handling and does not like to be pushed or forced into doing anything. He or she can be led and encouraged but will react stubbornly if driven. Aries children are adventurous and have no fear whatsoever.

The Aries woman is the traditional good woman behind the successful man. She is witty and charming and likes to look smart and attractive. Regardless of how successful her husband is, she will want to do something for herself and is very capable of doing so.

The Aries man tends to be distinguished in his appearance and always has somewhere to go and someone to see. He is always busy and is capable of being in charge of several things at one time. He likes his partner to be smart, good looking and considerate of his needs. He has a healthy appetite in all aspects of his life and needs to feel fulfilled.

Things to avoid are restlessness, anger and a tendency to act impulsively.

Famous People who share your sign are actors Marlon Brando, Charlie Chaplin and Sir Alec Guinness and Soviet premier Nikita Khrushchev.

Taurus ♉
The Second Sign of The Zodiac: 21 April–20 May

Born under the Earth sign of Taurus, a fixed sign that is ruled by Venus, your fortunate gemstones are amethyst, diamond sapphire and moss agate. Friday is your best day of the week and the colours red/orange and blue, and the numbers one and nine will be fortunate to you. Your most fortunate location to live or work is anywhere that is quiet, and your best choice of occupation is in the fields of the arts, drama and music, cosmetics and the land. You are most compatible with the signs Taurus, Cancer, Scorpio, Capricorn, Virgo and Pisces but you do not favour the signs of Aries, Gemini, Libra, Leo, Sagittarius and Aquarius.

You have an easy-going personality until you are crossed and then you become obstinate and headstrong. Your sign governs the ears, neck and throat, and any sensitivity will be present in those areas. Typical of the bull, you may have a tendency to indulge in all things pleasurable so you should exercise some control over what you eat and drink. If you are sensible with your diet, you will avoid many common ailments.

In affairs of the heart, you have to feel as though you are adored and if your loved one does not pay you enough attention, a dark cloud descends over you.

Your success will come through dedicated application and you have the patience and persistence to forge ahead when others would fall by the wayside.

The Taurus child is generally very even-tempered and

good-natured but they are quick to anger and can be very stubborn. They will, however, recognise their mistakes and learn from them. They are capable children and, although they mix well with others, they enjoy their own company.

The Taurus woman is affectionate and friendly. She makes a loyal partner and a devoted mother. She can be very determined and will be driven to achieve success or to assist her partner in achieving his. She needs material security in her life and will do all she can to develop it.

The Taurus man is dependable and very reliable. He generally exudes a sex appeal that makes him attract many female friends. He is supportive of his wife and family, and always puts them first. When single he will play the field with a healthy appetite but once he has chosen his partner he will be content and seldom strays. He has a great appreciation of beauty and likes to see this in his partner.

Things to avoid are jealousy, rage and a stubborn attitude.

Famous people who share your sign are artist Salvador Dali, singer Bing Crosby, dramatist William Shakespeare and Queen Elizabeth II.

Gemini ♊
The Third Sign of The Zodiac: 21 May–21 June

Born under the Air sign of Gemini, a mutable sign that is ruled by Mercury, your fortunate gemstones are emerald, tourmaline and lapis lazuli. The colours orange, silver and grey, and the numbers three and four will be lucky for you, and your best day of the week is Wednesday. The most fortunate location to live or work is anywhere that is high above sea level, and your best choice of occupations are in the fields of aviation, law, medicine, writing, printing, the media and travel. You are most compatible with the signs Aries, Gemini, Libra, Leo, Sagittarius and Aquarius, but you do not favour the signs of Taurus, Cancer, Scorpio, Capricorn, Virgo and Pisces.

You have a magnetic and attractive personality and will have many admirers. You enjoy the respect of others but can occasionally take people by surprise because of your short temper.

Your sign governs the hands, arms, chest and lungs and you should do your best to avoid coughs and colds. You can be inclined to overwork your mind and body and this can play havoc with your health too. In affairs of the heart, you are more likely to be stimulated by the mind of your lover rather than how he or she looks.

Your earning capacity will vary from time to time and you would be well advised to keep something by for rainy days. As a friend, you are interesting and you will have many acquaintances and a very active social life.

The Gemini child is curious and will keep you occupied answering questions about everything. They are very versatile and can handle almost anything, appearing to be little geniuses. The only thing that they find difficult is finishing what they have started and this is a skill which they have to be taught at an early age.

The Gemini woman is capable of running a home and a family with the same ease as someone who is running a business. She is meticulous in her approach to every job, large or small, and demands just reward for every effort that is made. If it comes to a battle of wits, she will win.

The Gemini man likes change and variety, and enjoys being many things to many people. He can work for an employer and run a small business on the side. He is usually very attractive and interesting to be with.

Things to avoid are restlessness and a tendency to be overconfident.

Famous people who share your sign are actress Marilyn Monroe, actress/singer Judy Garland, actor Errol Flynn and comedian/actor Bob Hope.

Cancer ♋
The Fourth Sign of The Zodiac: 22 June–22 July

Born under the water sign of Cancer, which is a Cardinal sign, your fortunate gemstones are pearl, moonstone aquamarine and sapphire. Your ruling planet is the Moon and the colours silver, white, yellow and orange are fortunate to you. Your best day of the week is Friday, and the numbers eight and three will be lucky for you. Your most fortunate location to live or work is close to water, and your best choice of occupations are in the fields of law, medicine, teaching, Engineering, catering, and the arts. You are most compatible with the signs of Taurus, Cancer, Leo, Scorpio, Capricorn and Pisces but you do not favour the signs of Aries, Gemini, Virgo Libra Sagittarius and Aquarius.

You have a quiet reserved personality and prefer a few loyal friends rather than many. Your sign governs the chest and stomach, and although you will have a strong constitution, you should maintain a healthy diet which will help you to guard against stomach disorders. You have a sensitive nervous system and should avoid worry, stress and depression. In affairs of the heart you are very affectionate and regard love as a serious matter. You will be totally devoted to your partner and easily roused to jealousy.

The Cancer child is receptive, imaginative and versatile. They can be timid and retiring, and are generally more comfortable in the home around family rather than mixing with newcomers and outsiders.

The Cancer woman can be quite difficult to get through to because of her crusty shell but she is the most motherly of all the signs. She is patient and devoted to the people she cares for and is very protective. She should guard against moodiness and depression, and overcome fear of achieving success.

The Cancer man is devoted to home and family but if too many demands are made on him he can turn into a nasty, old crab. He likes to spend a lot of time in and around the home and he likes it to be neat and tidy. His biggest fears are failure and poverty but he is likely to be successful. The Cancer man is very sensitive and easily hurt but he would never admit to this. If he is hurt in any way he will show his crusty exterior and this is almost impossible to penetrate.

Things to avoid are jealousy, spite, fear and gambling.

Famous people who share your sign are Roman Emperor Julius Caesar, actor James Cagney and jazz musician Louis Armstrong.

Leo ♌
The Fifth Sign of The Zodiac: 23 July–23 August

Born under the fire sign of Leo, which is a fixed sign, your fortunate gemstones are ruby, emerald and black onyx. Your ruling planet is the Sun and the colours yellow, gold and orange will be fortunate to you. Your best day of the week is Sunday and the numbers five and nine will be lucky for you. The most fortunate location to live or work is anywhere where there is lots of space around you, and your best choice of occupation is in the fields of politics, insurance, public utilities and production. You are most compatible with the signs Aries, Gemini, Libra, Leo, Sagittarius and Aquarius, but you do not favour the signs of Taurus, Cancer, Scorpio, Capricorn, Virgo and Pisces.

Although you are courteous and considerate you can be forceful and commanding and have the ability to influence others. Your sign governs the heart and bestows you with a generosity second to none. You have amazing recuperative abilities and can bounce back quickly when sickness befalls you. In affairs of the heart you can be very intense and are inclined to let your heart rule your head. Your earning capacity can be improved by cultivating a conservative attitude and overcoming a tendency to be free with your money. As a friend, you are entertaining and amusing and prefer to be at home with companions rather than socialising in the bright lights.

The Leo child is wilful, preferring to lead rather than

follow, but their pleasant nature tends to attract followers making it unnecessary for them to exert their dominance. They prefer to be outside, playing in wide-open spaces rather than being confined inside. When their tummies are full they are happy and content but they will be grumpy and fretful if they are hungry.

The Leo woman is passionate, attractive, and more often than not beautiful. Whatever she does, she puts her heart and soul into it. As a wife, she is a devoted partner but if her partner allows it, she will rule him to the limits of his endurance.

The Leo man is a very proud man and he likes his home and his family to reflect this. He is generous and kind but does not tolerate disloyalty or disobedience under any circumstances. He is the ruler of his pride of lions and demands to be treated as such. He is not easily fooled by anyone and does not suffer fools gladly.

Things to avoid are egotistical and impulsive behaviour.

Famous people who share your sign are political leader Napoleon Bonaparte, film producer/director Alfred Hitchcock and writer Sir Walter Scott.

Virgo ♍
The Sixth Sign of The Zodiac:
23 August –22 September.

Born under the Earth sign of Virgo, which is a mutable sign, your fortunate gemstones are diamond, jasper and sardonyx. Your ruling planet is Mercury and the colours grey, yellow and green, and the numbers eight and four will be lucky for you. Your best day of the week is Wednesday and the most fortunate location to live or work is a small city. Your best choice of occupation is in the fields of science, statistics, medicine, investments, publishing, promotions, property and anything to do with the land. You are most compatible with the signs Taurus, Cancer, Scorpio, Capricorn, Virgo and Pisces but you do not favour the signs of Aries, Gemini, Libra, Leo, Sagittarius and Aquarius.

As a friend you are you are trustworthy and diplomatic since you have a very good memory making you capable of examining all the facts and seeing both sides of any situation. You do not like being confined or restricted to small spaces and need freedom of movement to function to your fullest potential. Your sign governs the digestive organs and the intestine so you should look after your diet and get plenty of fresh air and sunlight. In affairs of the heart, you tend to be afraid to show your true feelings and suffer deeply if rejected. During your life, you will be presented with many opportunities to improve your finances and your success or failure will be depend on your dedication rather than good fortune. You are in control of your own destiny.

The Virgo child is intellectual and is best occupied with things that enable him or her to use their analytical capacities. They do not handle stress or worries well and will manifest them as illness. They can be very talented musically and if this is recognised early this ability can be nurtured through to success.

The Virgo woman can appear cold, insensitive and very reserved. In astrology, she represents the virgin and, for the most part, this is the image she portrays. Given the opportunity, however, she can show an entirely different nature if one finds herself in the right circumstances with people who she can truly trust. Her attitude to everything is business-like and she likes everything to be in its proper place.

The Virgo man has a picture in his head of what he wants and how he wants things to be. He will spend his life searching for these things and will accept them even if they do not make him happy. He is precise, organised and not prone to showing any emotion, but he can be a very good friend and a loyal worker.

Things to avoid are stress, worry and a tendency to over-react.

Famous people who share your sign are conqueror Alexander the Great, writer HG Wells and actress Sophia Loren.

Libra ♎
The Seventh Sign of The Zodiac:
23 September–22 October

Born under the Air sign of Libra, which is a Cardinal sign, your fortunate gemstones are opal, pink jasper, and chrysolite. Your ruling planet is Venus. The colours green and light blue, and the numbers six and nine will be lucky for you. Your best day of the week is Friday and the most fortunate location to live or work is anywhere where there is lots of social activity. Your best choice of occupation is in the fields of law, import and export, the armed forces, music and art. You are most compatible with the signs Aries, Gemini, Libra, Leo, Sagittarius and Aquarius, but you do not favour the signs of Taurus, Cancer, Scorpio, Capricorn, Virgo and Pisces.

Many of the most beautiful women and handsomest men are born under your sign. You are charming, often graceful, generous and loyal but with a word or a look can cut to the bone. You love the company of others but then, without much warning, you need your own space and have no difficulty in creating it.

Your sign governs the loins, kidneys and back and they reflect the most vulnerable areas in your body. Care should be taken to avoid depression, fatigue and moodiness. In affairs of the heart, you can be affectionate, tender and romantic but you do not always display your feelings. You are very selective when making friends and can take instant likes or dislikes to people but once you have accepted someone, you will be very loyal.

Financially, you can flirt between one extreme and the other, being a big spender one minute and behaving like a miser the next.

The Libra child must have his or her mind occupied at all times. When they are paying attention, they will do so one hundred percent, but if they are not interested, they will daydream and not hear a word you say. Libra children have strong artistic abilities and, when possible, this should be encouraged.

The Libra woman is often exotic in her appearance and attracts many friends and admirers, although she tends to be loyal to her partner. She likes to be surrounded by beautiful things and wants everything in her life to blend and balance.

The Libra man likes the excitement of the chase and, given the opportunity, he will sweep you off your feet like a knight in shining armour. He can be so charming and attentive that he could talk the birds out of the trees but, be warned, he can turn cold at the drop of a hat. When choosing his life partner the Libra man should do so carefully.

Things to avoid are excess and stress of any kind.

Famous people who share your sign are comedian/actor Groucho Marx, actress Brigitte Bardot and politician Eleanor Roosevelt.

Scorpio ♏
The Eighth Sign of the Zodiac:
23 October–22 November

Born under the water sign of Scorpio, which is a fixed sign, your fortunate gemstones are malachite, topaz and beryl. Some say that your ruling planet is Mars while others argue that it is Pluto. If you think before you act, Pluto is strong, but if you are more concerned with action rather than thinking about it, then Mars is your ruler. The colours green, blue and dark red, and the numbers three and five will be fortunate to you and your best day of the week is Tuesday. The most fortunate location for you to live or work is anywhere near water and you are capable of doing well in any choice of occupation but will excel in chemistry, medicine and surgery. You are most compatible with the signs Taurus, Cancer, Scorpio, Capricorn, Virgo and Pisces, but you do not favour the signs of Aries, Gemini, Libra, Leo, Sagittarius and Aquarius.

All the signs in the zodiac are easily recognisable by their traits with the exception of Scorpio. Taureans, for instance, particularly men, generally have thick necks and shoulders. Leos tend to have masses of hair, like the lion, or very short hair, which they fuss over constantly. But those who are born under the sign of Scorpio are not so easy to identify in terms of looks. Their particular trait is located in how they sound because they tend to talk a language of their own. Sometimes they like to sound poetic or mysterious. Your sign governs the reproductive areas of the body, making you the most sensuous, sexy and flirtatious sign in the zodiac. You have a magnetic, passionate personality and under normal circumstances you are considerate and loyal but you can have a very sharp and unexpected sting when roused to anger.

The Scorpio child likes to hide in small spaces just like a scorpion, and when these children are good they are very, very, good but when they are bad they can become little horrors. They like to have their own way and more often than not are determined to have the last word.

The Scorpio woman is not recognised for her tact or diplomacy. If she has something to say, she speaks her mind regardless of the consequences. She has a strong sexual appetite and makes a passionate partner.

The Scorpio man likes to rule the roost and can be very Victorian in his attitude towards his partner and children. He can be suspicious and jealous, guarding his possessions to the extreme. But if he can overcome this, he makes a loyal, loving and attentive partner.

Things to avoid are a sharp temper, restlessness and unreasonable jealousy.

Famous people who share your sign are artist Pablo Picasso, president Theodore Roosevelt and writer Robert Louis Stevenson.

Sagittarius ♐
The Ninth Sign of The Zodiac:
23 November–21 December.

Born under the Fire sign of Sagittarius, which is a mutable sign, your fortunate gemstones are turquoise, moonstone, and chrysolite. Your ruling planet is Jupiter, and the colours blue and purple, and the number nine will be fortunate to you. Your best day of the week is Thursday and the most fortunate location to live or work is the great outdoors. Your best choices of occupations are in the fields of travel, law, medicine, aviation, education, mechanics and writing. You are most compatible with the signs Aries, Gemini, Libra, Leo, Sagittarius and Aquarius but you do not favour the signs of Taurus, Cancer, Scorpio, Capricorn, Virgo and Pisces.

You are proud, independent and impulsive and dislike any kind of restriction, preferring to be a free spirit. You love adventure and travel, and given the opportunity will explore the universe. Your sign governs the thighs, and anything that involves movement, such as walking, running or dancing, will be important in your life. This influence will cause you to be restless in your nature and if you cannot fulfil your desire for travel, you will express it in other ways. You may move home many times or perhaps this will be reflected in your career. You should consider employment travelling as a salesperson or in the areas of seamanship, travel and tourism.

You have a nice personality and a good sense of humour and enjoy the respect and admiration of your friends. In affairs of the heart, you tend to be unsure of yourself one minute and overconfident the next. Choose your partner well because he or she will have to be able to put up with your restless nature.

The Sagittarius child is courageous and daring, and has a fiery, unpredictable temperament. These children are more likely to get into dangerous or difficult situations than other children are. They love animals and being outside, exploring.

The Sagittarius woman enjoys all types of outdoor activities and can be found participating in the more masculine sports such as hunting, fishing and riding. She loves activity of all kinds and has a real get-up-and-go attitude. She can bring out the best in her partner with very little effort. In the home, she is neat and tidy and she cares for her children well.

The Sagittarius man is interesting to know but difficult to pin down. He is an astute businessman and will be motivated by financial rewards rather than vocation. He tends not to be domesticated, preferring to leave that side of things to his partner or someone else. He is focused in his attitude and if something or someone no longer suits his purpose, he turns his back on them immediately.

Things to avoid are impulsive, thoughtless attitudes and a tendency to being bad tempered.

Famous people who share your sign are political leaders Sir Winston Churchill and Charles De Gaulle, and cartoonist and film producer, Walt Disney.

Capricorn ♑
The Tenth Sign of The Zodiac:
22 December–19 January

Born under the Earth sign of Capricorn, which is a Cardinal sign, your fortunate gemstones are onyx, ruby and garnet. Your ruling planet is Saturn, and the colours deep blue and dark green, in addition to the numbers seven and three will be fortunate to you. Your best day of the week is Saturday and the most fortunate location for you to live or work is a secluded, quiet place. Your best choice of occupation is in the fields of property, education, investigative journalism, writing and the land. You are most compatible with the signs Taurus, Cancer, Scorpio, Capricorn, Virgo and Pisces but you do not favour the signs of Aries, Gemini, Libra, Leo, Sagittarius and Aquarius.

You are trustworthy, dependable and loyal as a friend and will stand up for others who are unable to do so for themselves. Your sign governs the knees and, in order to maintain a healthy disposition, you should take regular, gentle exercise such as yoga rather than a hard workout. You will find success comes to you later in and, like the mountain goat, you will have some tough mountains to climb but you will get there in the end. You are persistent and stubborn and are not afraid of hard or repetitive work but, above all, you must feel fulfilled in what you do.

Given the choice of material success or job satisfaction you would probably choose the latter. In affairs of the heart, you are inclined to be reserved and reluctant to show your true feelings in case your love is rejected, but when your love is returned you lavish your partner with attention, tenderness and passion.

The Capricorn child is initially shy and reserved but as they get to know their peers, they become stronger and more confident. Friends they make in their early formative years tend to remember them in later years.

The Capricorn woman is strong in her principles and in her attitude, and it would be folly for anyone to try to dominate her. If she is dominated, it is only because she is allowing it. She is totally loyal and will do whatever is within her power to protect, encourage or direct her partner and children. She is businesslike in her approach to all matters whether this concerns family, home or romance. This can make her appear unfeeling at times but beneath this exterior lies a smouldering volcano.

The Capricorn man is the king and he expects all in his kingdom to obey him. Stick to this rule and you will be rewarded with support, love and encouragement. Break this rule and you will regret it. He can be miserly in his attitude and likes to maintain a tight rein on the bank balance, but, if he sees fit, can be very generous.

Things to avoid are pride, obstinacy and a selfish attitude.

Famous people who share your sign are martyr Joan of Arc, physicist Sir Isaac Newton and writer Rudyard Kipling.

Aquarius ♒
The Eleventh Sign of The Zodiac:
21 January–19 February

Born under the Water sign of Aquarius, which is a fixed sign, your fortunate gemstones are sapphire, jade, ruby and garnet. Your ruling planet is Uranus, and the colours indigo, pale blue and green, and the numbers eight and four will be fortunate to you. Your best day of the week is Wednesday and the most fortunate location for you to live or work is a large city, a place where there is a lot of activity. Your best choice of occupation is in the fields of aviation, exploration, electronics, politics and anything linked to sales and marketing. You are most compatible with the signs Aries, Gemini, Libra, Leo, Sagittarius and Aquarius but you do not favour the signs of Taurus, Cancer, Scorpio, Capricorn, Virgo and Pisces.

On first impression, you appear to be charming and courteous but you have a tendency to be offhand. You dislike pettiness, although this can be one of your own worst faults. You are the thinker of the zodiac and beneath your surface there is a lot going on that others would never guess at. You love excitement and what would appear to others as danger but the chances are that you will weighed things up before you act.

Your sign governs the calves and ankles, and exercise like hill-walking, climbing, aerobics or dancing will benefit you greatly and keep your constitution strong. In affairs of the heart you are easily hurt and hide your true feelings. Consequently, the object of your affections tends not to know how much you care.

As a friend you are loyal and supportive but can fall out of favour because of your hyper-critical attitude. Charming as you are, you always manage to find your way back into your companions' good books as though there was nothing wrong in the first place. Your earning capacity can be hampered by your vulnerability, which makes you easy prey for 'get-rich-quick-schemes'.

The Aquarius child is usually quite timid and will do whatever he or she is told. They do not handle any kind of stress well and need to feel safe at home and in their surrounding environment. They will be at their happiest with a good book full of adventure stories.

The Aquarius woman is independent, has a wide range of interests, and is capable of functioning on her own, having no need for masculine support. For this reason she is more likely to marry later in life and, although she will be loyal to her partner, if there is an important be reason to part, she will do so without hesitation.

The Aquarius man is a perfect gentleman most of the time. He treats everyone in the same way and is incapable of putting a lover or a partner on a pedestal, so don't hold your breath if this is what you want! Things to Avoid are criticism, thoughtlessness, aggression, selfishness and recklessness.

Famous people who share your sign are politicians Abraham Lincoln and Harold Macmillan and aviator Charles Lindbergh.

Pisces ♓
The Eleventh Sign of The Zodiac:
19 February–20 March

Born under the Water sign of Pisces, which is a mutable sign, your fortunate gemstones are moonstone, bloodstone, pearl and opal. Your ruling planet is Neptune, and the colour violet, in addition to the numbers five and eight will be fortunate to you. Your best day of the week is Friday and the most fortunate location for you to live or work is close to water.

Your best choice of occupation is in the fields of counselling, teaching, design, nursing, medicine, alternative therapies, aquatics and the arts. You are most compatible with the signs of Taurus, Cancer, Scorpio, Capricorn, Virgo and Pisces but you do not favour the signs of Aries, Gemini, Libra, Leo, Sagittarius and Aquarius.

You are kind, sympathetic and patient but are easily upset by others. You have a very soft nature and are easily led into bad company through trying your best to help and instead getting into tricky situations. Choose your friends wisely and do not believe every sob story that you hear.

Your sign governs the feet, the very foundation of your being. Keep them warm and dry to avoid colds, chills and throat infections.

As a friend, you would do without to help another and often regret it for seldom is this generosity returned. In affairs of the heart your feelings run deep but you are inclined to be in love with the idea of love rather than the person. This is when you are at your most vulnerable. Your financial security will depend on your ability to save wisely and make your money work for you rather than chancing your luck and speculating.

The Pisces child is easily impressed by the wrong company and should be taught discernment at an early age to help them avoid being manipulated later in life. They are studious by nature and have an amazing ability to retain anything they learn.

The Pisces woman is at her happiest when she is in restful, comfortable surroundings. Her home is her sacred space and, although she loves to be helpful and popular, too many demands weaken her spirit. She likes to socialise, be amongst acquaintances and generally have a good time but can only keep this pace up for a limited period and has to retreat back to her sacred space.

The Pisces man likes to have everything his own way. Where this becomes a problem is when he has a partner to consider because he can be very selfish. If his attributes are positive, he will be kind, considerate and caring, but if they are negative, he will be lazy and inconsiderate.

Things to avoid are mixing with the wrong type of people, and believing everything, you hear.

Famous People who share your sign are physicist Albert Einstein, inventor Alexander Graham Bell and actress Elizabeth Taylor.

Interpretations

Whether you are reading clouds in the sky, puddles in the ground or coffee in a saucer, the following interpretations will be helpful to you. Remember to trust your instincts, though, because things can have different meanings, associations or feelings for different people.

Abbey	A safe haven is being offered.
Acorns	Brings health, wealth, happiness and a joyful marriage.
Aeroplane	A journey is likely, for you or bringing someone to you. Changes will be experienced.
Alley	Indicates a loss of property or belongings.
Almond	A wedding.
Anchor	A symbol of safety and security.
Angel	This is a sign of safety and could be your guardian angel.
Anvil	Success and wealth, possibly through a new career.
Apples	Success in love, fertility, and growth in your life or business.
Archbishop	This can indicate a church service for a wedding or a funeral.

Interpretations

Arrow	This can be a warning of a threat to you, but if it is ornate it can be seen as an unknown admirer sending loving thoughts.
Axe	This can be threatening but is also the bringer of strength to handle difficult situations.
Baby	This is a sign of insecurity, a problem or responsibility, that you feel unable to deal with. A newborn baby can be a new beginning, as in a rebirth.
Bag	Although this is commonly a symbol for the womb, it can indicate hidden information.
Baggage	With too many problems to deal with, you are and feeling overburdened.
Bagpipes	A celebration of wealth and prosperity.
Balloon	Someone has grand schemes, which may not have the foundation required to make them successful.
Banner	A symbol of success in overcoming difficulty.
Battle	Indicates a difficult struggle ahead.
Beacon	Someone offers a solution or shows the way to solve a problem.
Beads	A sign of wealth to come.
Beard	This can represent someone who is trying to hide his or her true identity.
Bed	This can indicate that a rest is required to

regain strength and vitality. It can also suggest the need to avoid hasty action; wait or rest before doing something important.

Bells A warning to you that you are not heading your instincts.

Bicycle A leisurely journey will be made or there will be delays in progress.

Birds In a flock, birds can indicate that circumstances will change very suddenly and that the whole family will be affected. One bird represents a message waiting; two bring merriment or marriage; three indicates a successful journey; four suggests good news and five signifies company.

Bird's Nest If it contains eggs, this indicates growth and success, but if it is empty, a plan will fail.

Boat A journey across water will be made, or a letter or call will come from afar.

Bones This can indicate a problem that someone keeps going over, which cannot be resolved. Bones can also indicate a death or an ending.

Book An open book shows that the answer to your problem is staring you in the face. A closed book indicates that the answers that you seek may be harder to find, or that someone is keeping a secret from you.

Boots New boots are a symbol of material success but old boots indicate a previous lover returning.

Interpretations

Bottle	If the bottle is full you will be invited to share a celebration, if empty you will experience a disappointment.
Box	If the box is open and empty you will lose something or someone. If it is contains something, look up the contents in this list to find out what it means.
Bracelet	Happiness and success can be expected and a gift may be received.
Bride	You will hear of a wedding.
Bridge	You will experience a change in your life. (Broken: the opportunity for a change lies ahead but you would be better to avoid it.)
Bugle	Good news will arrive.
Buoy	Problems lie ahead but you will find a solution.
Burglar	Your possessions are threatened so be careful whom you trust or have around you at home or in the workplace.
Burial	You will finally be rid of a problem and you will hear of a birth.
Butcher	Do not take any chances or speculate as good luck is not with you.
Cage	You or a partner may feel trapped.
Candle	If the candle is bright then hope lies ahead if dim information is being concealed from you.
Candlestick	Religious ceremonies are significant.
Cannon	An important announcement will be made.

Canoe   Something that you are waiting for will be slow in arriving.

Car   An unexpected visitor will arrive if the car is facing towards you. If the car is facing away, you will make a journey.

Castle   A symbol of wealth suggesting you can look forward to a prosperous future.

Cave   You may wish you could hide away from your problems or responsibilities.

Chains   You are in danger if being manipulated into something that you would rather not be involved in.

Chair   The more ornate the chair, the more fortunate the omen.

Chalice   Perfect truth and love will come to you.

Children   If they are playing, you have a desire to be free of responsibilities and return to a time when things in your life were easier.

Chimney   A wedding will be announced.

Christ   To see the face of Christ indicates that you are being given help and support in an unseen way.

Church   A religious ceremony is imminent.

City   This could indicate that you are or will feel overwhelmed by a situation or responsibility.

Clock   This is generally a sign that time is passing and that you will have to be disciplined in order to achieve your desires.

Interpretations

Clown	Someone may be trying to hide his or her true identity or character from you. This is not a good omen.
Club	You will be involved in a very sensual relationship and this will prove to be a very fertile period for you or someone very close to you.
Coals	A very lucky symbol denoting warmth and success in your future.
Colours	**Black** is for grounding and dispelling negative energies. **Blue** is for tranquillity and peace. **Green** is for healing, growth and fertility. **Orange** is for strength, power and courage. **Pink** is for love and romance. **Purple** is for protection, meditation and spirituality. **Red** is for passion, excitement and action. **Turquoise** is for communication, protection and travel. **White** is for purity, cleansing and knowledge. **Yellow** is for energy, vitality and motivation.
Corkscrew	Someone may try to glean information from you or about you.
Cornucopia	Good news is on the way.
Corridor	You will have to make a choice or a decision very soon.
Crescent	This is a very feminine symbol depicting

	involvement, or very good news from someone of the female sex.
Cross	Burdens may be heavy but look within to find solutions.
Crossroads	A choice will have to be made and it must be made alone.
Crown	You will be recognized for an achievement.
Crutches	Help will be offered from an unexpected source.
Cupid	Someone is thinking of you romantically.
Dagger	You may or may have been betrayed in love.
Devil	This depicts fear of making decisions or choices, or of making a commitment.
Dice	The choice ahead will depend entirely on luck, good or bad.
Doormat	A visitor will arrive unexpectedly.
Doors	If the door is open a new opportunity will be offered. If the door is closed you will not get what you want.
Drum	An important announcement will be made and you may not be happy with what you hear.
Eggs	Birth or new beginnings that show great potential.
Enclosure	This can be a sign that there is no way to avoid a problem and that you must face up to it and deal with it.
Execution	There will be an unfortunate outcome to a plan or endeavour.

Interpretations

Explosion	Be prepared for an outburst of some kind.
Eyes	You are being watched or observed. This could be for promotion in your career or for other reasons.
Fairy	A fortunate symbol showing that the elements are on your side and will help where they can.
Fan	Although in some cultures this is the symbol for wealth and royalty, it can also show that a situation is in danger of becoming over-heated.
Feathers	Your ideas may not be as strong as you suppose and some additional information may be required.
Fields	An indication that you have many choices and can go anywhere or do anything.
Finger	You are being pointed in the right direction so listen to advice that is offered.
Fire	You will begin to regain your strength and vitality.
Flowers	Each flower has a specific meaning so look at the Flower List (pp 205) for an accurate description.
Gallows	You are heading in the wrong direction and may fall from a great height if you proceed.
Garden	The more abundant the garden, the more fortunate the meaning.

Interpretations

Garlands	A fortunate omen showing that you will succeed in your endeavours.
Gate	If the gate is open then the way ahead is clear and you can proceed with confidence. If the gate is blocked in any way then your progress will be blocked too.
Gems	An indication that you will be spoiled or pampered in some way.
Genitals	You are entering a very fertile period in your life and should make the most of it.
Ghosts	Something from your past will come back to haunt you.
Giants	Someone who is much older than you will have words of advice to offer, even if you do not want to hear them.
God	This is a very profound symbol regardless of your religion, and shows that your God is watching over you and communicating with your intellect.
Gondola	News from a foreign country will arrive.
Grapes	Recovery in health matters and good fortune in financial or material affairs.
Grotto	A place of worship and spirituality showing that you must develop your spiritual side and listen to your heart.
Guitar	You may be invited to a friendly gathering and participate in a celebration.
Gun	You will be protected from opposition.

Interpretations

Hair	A feminine symbol, 'a woman's crowning glory'. It shows the desire to be viewed as a feminine and graceful woman, or to have a beautiful woman as a partner.
Hair	**Black, short hair:** official business that may be difficult to handle. **Dishevelled:** problems can be expected unless you put your affairs in order. **Long, flowing free:** indicates, freedom from burdens. **White:** news or advice from an elder.
Hammer	This can be an indication that you will be provided with the tools to achieve your goals, but the going will be difficult.
Hands	Help will be offered.
Hanging	You may feel as though you are in a state of suspended animation and that nothing can change this, but sudden changes for the better will be experienced.
Heart	Romance is on your mind and you may be wishing that you had someone in your life.
Harvesters	Wealth will come to you.
Hatchet	Beware of treachery and deceit.
Hawk	Pay close attention to small details to avoid missing essential information.
Hay-cart	Prosperity in affairs to do with finances, land or property.
Hermit	Someone will show you a new way of life.

Interpretations

Honey   A fortunate omen indicating prosperity.

Horseshoe If the open end of the horseshoe faces upwards then this is a very lucky omen, but if the open ends are facing down you are in danger of losing something precious, and good fortune is not with you.

House   If the house is standing strong then you are in a good position to deal with matters. If the house is dilapidated and falling down then you are at a weak point in your life and need the support of friends or loved ones.

Ice or Frost A warning that you are about to make a mistake. Exercise caution in all areas of your life.

Iceberg This could be an indication that you are only being made aware of some of the facts pertaining to a situation, person or issue. More is hidden below the surface.

Ice skates With more experience you will be able to handle a difficult situation. Look to those who have experience for the answers.

Igloo   You are looking for a safe haven.

Indian   This may indicate that guidance is being offered and that you should look to your elders for this.

Initials   An important matter is connected to someone who has the initial in their name.

Ink Blot The interpretation is dependent on the

Interpretations

	shape or form of the blot.
Island	You may feel as though you are having to stand alone and face all the difficulties that life and destiny is throwing your way.
Jester	Someone may give you false information.
Jolly Roger	This is a warning that danger lurks nearby.
Judge	You may be questioning something in your life and wonder what others may think of this.
Jug	A time to celebrate is close.
Kettle	You will have unexpected guests.
Key	A new home or opportunity will be offered to you
Kite	This is a desire to be free.
Knife	You will have the power, strength and ability to sever ties if necessary and forge ahead.
Knight	(in armour) Although problems may lie ahead, solutions will be found through the intervention of another.
Knots	This can be an indication that you feel as though you are tied in knots but others may experiences this as goals to be accomplished.
Ladder	New openings will occur but although the goal may be difficult to achieve, it is likely to be achieved providing you maintain a steady attitude and disciplined effort.

Interpretations

Lamp or Lantern	You will be shown the answers that you require.
Leaves	This can be a sign that you feel as though your plans are falling apart.
Letter	Important news is on the way.
Lighthouse	A solution will be found or hope will be offered.
Logs	A sign of warmth and security.
Mask	Treachery or deception is around so be wary who you trust.
Maypole	You will be involved in a very physically exciting relationship.
Medal	This could be described as a desire for praise.
Mill	You will begin to reap rewards from the efforts that you have made.
Money	An indication that money may be coming to you from an unexpected source.
Monsters	You may have an underlying fear that must be faced before you realize that you had nothing to fear.
Moon	Beware of deception and depression.
Mother	This indicates that you are well protected and can proceed without fear
Mountain	Obstacles lie ahead but they can be overcome by looking for an alternative route or path to your goals.
Mouth	News will come and it may take the form of gossip or scandal.

Interpretations

Necklace	Guard your tongue as what you say may be misunderstood.
Needle	Beware of sharp objects or of annoying someone close to you.
Nest	You will be asked to care for a child or a pet.
Net	You could become caught up in an unsavory or difficult situation.
Nose	You may find something or find out about something.
Nuts	Rewards will be bestowed for efforts made.
Oasis	You will find a safe haven.
Obelisk	Fame and fortune will arrive for efforts and application already made.
Old woman	Guidance and inspiration will be given in answer to a prayer.
Orchestra	A time of great happiness lies ahead.
Organ	A wedding will be announced.
Oven	Someone close to you is planning something but keeping their plans to themselves.
Padlock	You will be unable to discover the answer to a mystery or puzzle.
Palace	You will find the answers that you seek and you will also find your destiny.
Paper	Someone or something is trying to give you information that you need.
Parcel	You will learn something new.
Path	You will find a new direction to follow. How easy or difficult it is depends entirely

on the shape of the path, the smoother and wider, the easier your transition will be.

Pawnbroker You may lose something of value or importance but will be able to substitute it with something else.

Pen You will receive news.

Penis A very powerful man will come into your life.

Phoenix Good health will be restored to someone dear to you who is ill.

Pies A party or gathering will be organized to celebrate an event.

Pillow Someone may need to rest due to illness or injury.

Pincers Be prepared for a betrayal.

Pipe A disagreement will be resolved.

Pirate An untrustworthy character will try to involve you in something shady although you may not realize this at the time.

Pistol You will be protected from opposition..

Pitcher You will have to work very hard to achieve your goals and no one will be willing to help you.

Pitchfork You are in a very dangerous position

Plough News of a pregnancy will arrive and you could be entering a very fertile period in your life.

Police   Uniforms and legal matters will be important.

Pool   Water is cleansing, healing and refreshing so if the pool is clear, good health can be expected, but if the pool is murky, sickness is close.

Portrait   You are being watched from afar.

Precipice   You may be afraid to take a chance.

Priest   Someone will show you a new way of life, and a prayer will be answered.

Prison   You may feel trapped in your present situation but release will come soon.

Prize   You may receive a reward or recognition for something that you have done.

Procession   A wedding or anniversary celebration will be announced.

Purse   You will be guarding your possessions and may feel threatened in a personal way.

Pyramid   You will achieve a cherished goal.

Quayside   A journey will be made and the parting will be sad.

Queen   You will be successful in your ambitions and reach the top of your chosen career.

Question mark   Someone will seek your advice.

Radio   You will hear news from afar.

Raft   Do not make any changes at this time, because luck is not with you.

Railway   A journey will be made.

Interpretations

Rainbow	This is a sign of hope for the future.
Reeds	You will have obstacles to overcome but if you are persistent, you will overcome them.
Rider	You will be swept off your feet in an exciting, romantic adventure.
Ring	A wedding or divorce will be announced, depending on the condition of the ring.
Road	You will find a new direction to follow. How easy or difficult depends entirely on the shape of the road. The smoother and wider, the easier your transition will be.
Rock	No one will move you from your chosen path.
Rocket	You will make progress faster than you anticipate.
Roof	You will reach the top in your chosen profession.
Rope	You may be reluctantly entwined or involved in something.
Rowing	Progress will be made but it may be slower than you would hope.
Ruins	You will rebuild from scratch and rebuild in strength.
Sailor	A journey across water will be made.
Scarecrow	There are people around you who cannot be trusted.
Scissors	If the scissors are open beware of quarrels and arguments, if they are closed,

	arguments and disagreements will be resolved.
Scroll	You will receive a message from an unexpected source.
Scythe	A relationship will be severed.
Sentinel	You will be protected during both your sleeping and waking hours.
Seraphim	You will learn something to your advantage from someone much younger than you.
Shelter	Problems may lie ahead but you will be protected from them.
Shepherd	Someone will show you a new direction. Take it!
Ship	A journey will be made to a far-off place.
Shipwreck	Your plans will not go as you would wish.
Shirt	Official matters will go well if the shirt is whole and badly if the shirt is crushed or damaged.
Shoes	You have become discontent with your present situation are be longing for pastures new.
Sieve	You will lose your belongings or security if you do not exercise care and caution.
Skeleton	All pretence will be stripped away and plain speaking will win the day.
Skull	You are under threat of losing a hope, dream or possession.
Soldiers	Help will be offered but only if you ask.
Spade	You will have to work very hard to achieve your goal.

Spear	Someone may stab you in the back, betray you or speak ill of you.
Spectacles	You may be unaware of all the facts so ask more questions.
Steps	You will rise to great heights.
Sugar	You will be flattered and praised, and enjoy being the centre of attention.
Sun	Your daily life will begin to improve.
Sundial	Make better use of your time.
Swimmer	You have almost reached your goal but not quite. More effort is required.
Sword	You will be given more power to cut through your obstacles and overcome adversity.
Table	Your material security will be strengthened.
Tambourine	Good fortune will bless you and you will celebrate with others.
Tassels	An official ceremony will be organized and you may be required to attend this.
Teapot	Unexpected guests will arrive and a stranger will be brought to your home.
Tears	Although you may shed some tears they will not be ones of sadness.
Teeth	All is not well. Guard your health.
Telephone	News will arrive that will excite you.
Temple	You will experience some kind of mystical illumination.
Tent	You may be worried about your stability and security. Exercise caution in financial matters.

Interpretations

Thermometer Unexpected changes will upset your plans.

Thighs The sign of Sagittarius may be significant.

Thimble A period of unemployment may be experienced.

Throne You will be praised and respected for your knowledge and experience.

Tinker Problems with neighbours can be expected.

Tomb You will find that you are stuck in a rut and unable to make any progress.

Torch You will be reminded of a past love.

Torpedo News will come that will shock or upset you.

Tower A crisis will unfold and nothing that you say or do can change this.

Train A decision will have to be made and the choice must be yours and yours alone.

Trapdoor Hidden information will be revealed.

Trench Beware of hidden obstacles.

Triangle You will hear of someone who is having an affair.

Tripod Your plans are not as secure as you would suppose.

Trumpet Someone will boast bout his or her possessions or achievements.

Trunk A house move is likely.

Tub Problems lie ahead.

Tunnel You will have a fresh start.

Umbrella You will be protected from a difficult situation or person.

Undertaker You will hear of a birth.

Unicorn You will achieve your dreams.

Urn You will hear of a death or a sudden misfortune concerning another.

Vagabond You will move home and it will be the first of several moves before you finally settle down.

Valley You will experience a delay in achieving your desires.

Vase You may feel as though no one cares and that you have to do everything yourself.

Veil You are uncomfortable about expressing your self or your desires.

Victory Salute You will be successful in your attempts to overcome obstacles.

Village You will wish that your life were more settled and content.

Violin You will be invited to a party.

Volcano There will be violent outbursts and quarrels.

Wading Good health will be restored.

Wall Barriers will be difficult to overcome in your personal, professional or romantic life.

Watch Good fortune will come but it may be slow in arriving.

Water Bearer The sign of Aquarius is important.

Water Mill Good health will be restored and good fortune will follow.

Waves Be patient, what you want will come to

Interpretations

you but if you force things now you will upset the outcome.

Wedding You may be wishing for romantic fulfilment.

Whale You will have the answer that solves another's problem.

Wharf While others around you may panic, you will be calm in the knowledge that all will be well.

Wheel You are about to experience a complete change in your life.

Whip Someone may threaten your peace of mind.

Whirlpool Unnecessary changes will bring disaster.

Whirlwind Unnecessary changes will lead to your downfall so allow things to remain as they are for the time being.

Wig Someone is showing you a false side to their nature and you are in danger of being taken in by this.

Windmill Changes for the better will surprise you.

Window You will hear of or be involved in a scandal.

Wings You will have the desire to escape from your everyday life.

Witch You will experience a stroke of unexpected good luck.

Wreath You will win an argument or a battle.

Wreck Good fortune may escape you so exercise caution in all your dealings.

Interpretations

Yacht   Progress will be quick or slow depending
             on the assistance that is offered or withheld.

**Zodiac
Symbols**   These generally depict someone who is
             born under that sign or something
             associated with it.

Creatures Great and Small

Alligator   A dangerous enemy.

Ants   A successful project which others will assist with.

Ape   This can be either good or bad depending on the image. It can indicate a strong ally or an enemy

Bear   An indication that you will find the answers that you seek within yourself. This inner wisdom will show you the way forward.

Bees   They can indicate a source of riches or sustenance, but if the bees are threatening or swarming you will be attacked from an unexpected source.

Beetles   Indicate someone who is hard on the outside but vulnerable inside, or someone who is trying to hide something.

Boar   A threat lies ahead, be careful who you trust.

Bull   An unexpected windfall or an amorous lover will arrive, and the sign of Taurus will be significant.

Butterfly   You will emerge from a difficult situation wiser and stronger.

Creatures Great and Small

Camel	You will have the ability to continue with a responsibility, task or aim even though the going may be difficult.
Cat	If the appearance of the cat is friendly then good fortune is around. If the cat appears aggressive then beware of jealousy. A new-found freedom could be the key to your future.
Cat	(Black) A sign of good luck if the cat appears to be resting or friendly. If the cat is threatening, problems that will be difficult to deal with lie ahead. (White) You are being given a warning.
Cattle	Indicate prosperity.
Chameleon	You are being deceived or are deceiving yourself.
Clam	This a good omen.
Cock	Someone will boast of his or her achievements to the annoyance of others.
Cow	A symbol of wealth, spiritual attainment and material abundance.
Crab	You may experience someone's anger.
Crocodile	Be careful of the company you keep as you may be associating with a dangerous enemy.
Dog	You will hear from a good friend, or a friend will help in time of need.
Dolphin	Someone close can be trusted to provide help or answers.

Creatures Great and Small

Donkey   You will be given assistance in moving home, or will offer to help someone changing address.

Dragon   A very lucky symbol in relationships, wealth and happiness.

Elephant   Known for its memory, the elephant will show you that what you seek lies within your own power to remember. Look deeper and you will find the answers.

Elk   This will bring you strength in times of need and is also the symbol of friendship.

Ermine   A symbol of wealth with royal connections.

Fawn   A symbol depicting innocence, and since the mother is usually nearby her fawn, protection is close at hand.

Ferret   Keep looking, with perseverance you will find what you seek.

Fish   The birth of a child will be announced.

Fox   You will have the ability to see and not be seen in order to find the answers that you are looking for.

Frogs   A spiritual, emotional or physical cleansing is required.

Goat   Keep trying to achieve your goals and, like the goat, climb to new and higher levels. The sign of Capricorn may be significant.

Goose   This is a symbol of male fertility and wealth.

Creatures Great and Small

Grasshopper You will be unable to focus on any specific task and will hop from one situation to another.

Hare Look for opportunities in strange or unusual surroundings.

Hedgehog You or your space may be threatened by outside influences.

Horse In Native American tradition, the horse is a symbol of power so seeing this animal is indicative of power or support coming to you.

Hyena You will hear of a robbery.

Insect An irritating problem may bother you.

Kangaroo This can be in indication that you feel responsible for someone younger than you who is unable to look after themself.

Kitten A desire to have someone or something to cherish and care for.

Lambs A hope for the future to be prosperous and secure.

Leopard You may have to be very cunning to achieve a desire, or information that is important to you.

Lion A very important person will be introduced to you and the sign of Leo is important.

Lizard You will have a prophetic experience that will safeguard you in some way.

Lobsters Generally bodes sorrow but fans of the TV programme 'Friends' may see this as the arrival of a soulmate.

Creatures Great and Small

Lynx	You or your actions are being observed.
Mice	Be wary of overindulging in food drink or self-gratification.
Monkey	Deceit and treachery are around and you may find something that you consider to be serious is laughed at.
Mushrooms	What appears to be a small unimportant idea may in fact be the solution to a problem.
Otter	Do not trust strangers.
Oysters	There may be some tears ahead for you or someone close to you
Ox	You will be tied to your responsibilities for a while yet.
Panther	This is a warning that danger lies ahead.
Pig	You may find that you have to search long and hard to find what you are looking for.
Porcupine	If you are careful you will be able to handle a difficult situation.
Porpoise	Joy and happiness will come to you.
Rabbit	You are afraid of something or someone and should rid yourself of this fear, because it is unnecessary.
Racoon	You will gather and reorganize your belongings.
Ram	The sign of Aries will be significant.
Rat	You will be cunning and clever, and find the solution to a problem.
Reindeer	A celebration is at hand and your friends will gather around you.

Creatures Great and Small

Reptile   Be wary, there is someone near you whom you should not trust.

Salmon   You will achieve your goals.

Scorpions   The sign of Scorpio will be important.

Serpent   You will experience a complete transformation.

Shark   There are hidden dangers around you be careful.

Sheep   Make your own decisions rather than following the decisions that others make.

Snail   Wealth and success will come to you if you take your time and be diligent in your attempts.

Spider   You will learn a new subject and from your learning you will change radically.

Stag   A successful businessman will assist you and may have more than business on his mind.

Tiger   An enemy is waiting to foil your plans. Keep them to yourself to avoid danger.

Toad   You will meet someone that you will instantly take a dislike to.

Tortoise   Success can be achieved by persistent effort.

Trout   Unexpected money will arrive.

Walrus   You are wasting your time and abilities. Do something radical and you will find fulfilment.

Wasp   You will experience a sudden quarrel from an unexpected source.

Creatures Great and Small

Weasel   Someone who pretends to be a friend is really an enemy in disguise.

Wildcat   An unexpected confrontation will be experienced among your circle of friends.

Wolf   You will teach others or study a new subject.

Zebra   Someone will be stronger and more reliable than you had at first thought.

Specific Types of Birds

Albatross	This is a warning of danger ahead.
Blackbird	Expect trouble and possibly a threat to your reputation.
Bluebird	You will meet a cheerful fellow.
Chicken	You will hear gossip.
Crane	Someone will try to take something from you.
Crossbill	An argument is imminent.
Crow	One crow for sorrow, two crows for mirth, three crows for a wedding and four crows for birth.
Cuckoo	A guest may wish to stay overnight or may overstay their welcome.
Dove	An argument will be settled or a broken mended.
Duck	One duck means a period of solitude can be expected, but two ducks indicate happiness in a relationship.
Eagle	This is a symbol of power and protection, and gives the ability to see problems from a different angle to help find a solution.
Falcon	A symbol of power over your enemies.
Geese	A fortunate omen indicating that good luck

Specific Types of Birds

	will come from an unexpected source. News will come from or for your mother.
Goldfinch	You will be entertained or admired by a wealthy suitor.
Hawk	You will receive a message that will bring enlightenment.
Humming bird	The symbol of joy and freedom of choice.
Jackdaw	You will have important mail or documents to attend to.
Kingfisher	Peace of mind and contentment will be yours.
Lapwing	News will come from afar.
Lark	You will celebrate within the week.
Magpie	

'One for sorrow,
Two is for joy.
Three for a girl,
Four is for a boy.
Five for silver,
Six is for gold.
Seven for a secret,
Never to be told.'

Another old rhyme says:
'One means anger,
Two brings mirth.
Three is a wedding,
Four is a birth.

Specific Types of Birds

Five is christening,
Six is a dearth.
Seven is heaven,
Eight is Hell,
But nine is the very Devil's ain sel.'

Martin	Good luck around the home.
Ostrich	Do not hide from your problems but deal with them head on.
Owl	A mentor will provide the answers that you seek.
Parrot	Someone will betray you so do not divulge your secrets.
Partridge	You are likely to make a very silly mistake.
Peacock	A wealthy marriage or partnership.
Pheasant	Success and security will be yours.
Pigeon	You will be surprised by someone's unconventional behaviour.
Raven	Legal and business matters will be discussed and others will be responsible for the outcome.
Robin	Contentment around the home, news from an old friend, and you will make a new friend.
Rook	Pay attention to any rumours or stories and what you hear may surprise you.
Sparrow	Children, young pets or plants may need your attention.
Stork	News of a birth will arrive.
Swallow	News from afar is forecast.

Creatures Great and Small

Swan	(White) Contentment and love. Wealth and happiness to come. **(Black)** Sadness to follow.
Turkey	A celebration.
Vulture	Others may view you with envy.
Woodpecker	You will spend time alone.
Wren	A small package will delight you.

Things That Grow

Acacia   You will overcome obstacles; this tree is associated with the sign of Aries.

Alder   You will begin to see things more clearly and the sign of Pisces is important.

Almond   Virgo will be significant and you will be required to be more organised in order to achieve success.

Angelica   Good health will be restored.

Apple   A problem on the home front will be solved. Taurus will be important.

Ash Tree   Legal matters will progress smoothly and the sign of Libra will be significant.

Bamboo   Quarrels and arguments can be expected.

Bananas   The fruit of the gods can indicate a blessing or a curse from above.

Basil   Courage will be with you when it is required and money will arrive.

Bay   Success will be achieved.

Bergamot   Success will be achieved

Birch   A fresh start will be offered and Sagittarius is significant.

Blackthorn You are being warned to keep your secrets to yourself; Scorpio is associated witht his traditional hedging tree.

Things That Grow

Borage   Advice will be offered and should be taken.

Carnation   Peace, contentment and restful nights.

Cedar   Healing to someone who is sick, and news from an eastern country.

Cedarwood   You or someone you care for will be protected from harm.

Chamomile   Success will be yours.

Cherry   You are being advised to stand your ground; the sign of Aquarius is associated with this tree.

Chervil   You may study a new subject.

Chives   Courage will come to you when you need it.

Cinnamon   An unexpected windfall will arrive.

Clover   Lady luck will be with you in a speculative venture.

Comfrey   Good luck in overcoming obstacles.

Coriander   Good health will be yours.

Corn   This is a good omen indicating plenty to come.

Cypress   You may start again in a new place but will be sorry to leave your present one; the sign of Taurus may be important.

Daffodils   Health and happiness to follow.

Daisy   A time of brightness and celebration to follow.

Dill   Money will come soon.

Elder   You will have a prophetic or telepathic experience and the sign of Pisces will be important.

Things That Grow

Elm	You are being told that help will be offered when you need it most; Capricorn is associated with the Elm.
Fennel	You will make an unexpected journey.
Fern	You will have good luck in overcoming obstacles.
Feverfew	You will be blessed with joy and family happiness.
Fig	Pisces is associated with this tree and you are being told that someone will recover from a serious illness.
Frankincense	You will be blessed with joy and family happiness. You will be given protection from harm or harmful people.
Gardenia	Love and romance will be the focus of your attention.
Garlic	You will be given protection from harm or harmful people or energies.
Geranium	Courage will be with you.
Ginger	Money will arrive soon.
Grapefruit	The sign of Aquarius may be important and you are being told to think carefully before you make the choice that lies ahead.
Hawthorn	You are being given the protection of a guide on the astral plane; hawthorn is associated with the sign of Aries.
Hazel	You are being granted peace of mind and contentment; Gemini is associated with this tree.

Things That Grow

Heather	Good luck will be with you and you will overcome obstacles. You may feel frustrated in your attempts to change something but be persistent and you will win through in the end.
Hemlock	Danger is present so exercise caution in all that you do.
Hibiscus	You will have a psychic experience or prophetic dream.
Holly	This is the symbol of joy and brings news of good times to come.
Honeysuckle	This is the symbol for courage during difficult times.
Horse	Chestnut Expect quarrels and arguments.
Hyacinth	Good fortune can be expected. Good news will arrive concerning a member of your family.
Hyssop	Take care of your health and try to avoid chills, fevers and colds.
Ivy	The hand of friendship will be offered and can be accepted.
Jasmine	True love will be yours to embrace.
Juniper	Good health is forecast and good luck will be with you always.
Laurel	You will win a competition, raffle or a prize for your efforts.
Lavender	A new friend will be made.
Lemon	Peace of mind and contentment will be yours.
Lemongrass	You spirituality will be enhanced.

Things That Grow

Lilac	You will be protected from harmful influences or situations.
Lilies	Someone will be proved innocent of a crime. (Tiger) You may be tempted by envy or greed. (Water) Someone will recover from a troublesome illness.
Lily of the Valley	You will be shy about accepting praise that you do not think you deserve.
Lime	This will bring news from or a visitor from a far off place; lime is associated with the sign of Sagittarius.
Lotus	This is the symbol of new beginnings.
Marigold	This plant will bring success to new ventures and a happy marriage.
Marjoram	You will spend a few days away from home for business or social reasons.
Meadowsweet	Peace and contentment will be yours.
Mimosa	Love and romance will find you.
Mint	You will have a happy home.
Mistletoe	An admirer will compliment you.
Morning glory	You will find good reason to be hopeful.
Mulberry	An increase of wealth; this bush is associated with the sign of Sagittarius.
Myrrh	Brings happiness and contentment.
Nettle	Take advantage of opportunities that come your way but handle them with care.
Nutmeg	Good luck will come and help you overcome obstacles.

Things That Grow

Oak	The sign of Sagittarius is significant and you will be able to establish your independence one way or another.
Olive	An apology will be made and accepted.
Onion	Be wary of new people who may try to ingratiate themselves into your circle.
Orchard	If abundant the signs are good, if barren then your plans will fail.
Palm	You will have a successful outcome to a project or plan and a wedding will be announced; palms are associated with the sign of Leo and will bring victory.
Pansy	Your loved one will be true to you.
Peaches	You will be wined, dined and entertained.
Pepper	You will have the ability to dispel any negative influences.
Pine	Associated with the sign of Capricorn and will bring Good fortune and good health.
Pineapple	You will be invited to a celebration or a wedding.
Poplar	Associated with the sign of Libra and will bring an awareness and insight that will lead to justice.
Poppy	Good health will be yours.
Potatoes	You will reap the rewards of the efforts that you have made.
Primroses	Sad or upsetting news will come to you.
Pumpkin	You will have many admirers and be popular as a friend.

Things That Grow

Raspberries	You will receive news of a birth.
Rose	Love and romance will find you.
Rosemary	Success will be yours if you stay focused.
Rye	You will win an argument.
Sage	You will learn from someone who has wisdom, experience and knowledge.
Shamrock	You will cross water.
Sorrel	You will find the love that you are looking for.
Strawberries	You will have a good life and a happy marriage.
Sweet Pea	Success will be well earned and appreciated.
Sycamore	A wedding invitation will arrive.
Tansy	True love will find a way.
Thistle	A problem will have to be handled with care.
Thyme	You will embark on an education programme and you will probably be the teacher.
Toadstool	Speedy progress will be made concerning your plans for the future.
Tomato	Happiness may be slow to come and may not last long.
Turnip	You will have an unexpected advancement or windfall.
Vanilla	Romance will come to you.
Vetivert	Good luck will be with you and romance will follow.
Vines	Abundance will be yours

Things That Grow

Violet	You will learn something new and interesting
Walnut	Beware of treachery.
Watermelon	Guard your health
Wheat	You will receive an unexpected windfall.
Willow	You or someone close to you will shed tears. The sign of Cancer will be important.
Wisteria	A happy marriage is forecast.
Yew	Associated with the sign of Capricorn, this tree brings honour and great wealth.

The Crystal List

Agates
Agates come in a variety of colours and will help to eliminate negativity and cleanse the aura.

Agate Blue Lace
This pale blue stone has delicate markings in white, which usually have a lace effect, hence the name. It helps with communication and eases pain caused by breaks, sprains, fractures and arthritis.

Agate Moss
I have a piece that is completely clear with very well-defined pieces of fossilised moss within it, but moss agate is generally dark green with coloured markings. This is a stone that can be used to build your inner strength and stabilise your emotions.

Amber
This is one of my favourites and comes in shades ranging from the palest yellow, through green and red to the deepest brown. Amber is fossilised resin and in days gone by it would have been crushed and powdered to make a healing potion.

Amber brings good luck and protects the bearer from

harm. I wore a gold amber necklace on my wedding day and only discovered afterwards that it is known as a symbol for renewing wedding vows and making promises.

It brightens the spirit, lifts depression and has been successfully used in the treatment of throat, kidney and bladder problems.

Amethyst

This is traditionally known as the elevator stone because it gives you a 'lift' and hence aids depression. A fabulous all-round healer, amethyst comes in many varieties and shades of lilac through to purple. It relieves tension and stress, and helps to give the bearer insight into situations that require a decision.

It can be used to improve posture and is commonly used for arthritis. For insomnia, place a piece of amethyst under your pillow or hold a piece in your hand as you go to sleep. Keep amethyst on you to enhance telepathy.

Ametrine

A mixture of amethyst and citrine, it combines qualities of both stones. Ametrine brings balance to the male and female qualities, stimulates the intellect in meditation and helps us to find peace and tranquillity.

Aquamarine

This is the stone you need to 'always be prepared'. Its gentle energy helps judgemental people to be more tolerant, and those who get swamped with responsibility to stand up for themselves, whilst also bringing order to chaos.

Aventurine
A stone for the heart, it calms troubled emotions, attracts prosperity, and is a lucky stone. It helps enhance leadership qualities and strengthens the instinctive part of your nature. Bloodstone

Use to revitalize love and friendship and to benefit the internal workings of the body. As its name suggests, it keeps the blood healthy and helps in blood-related diseases.

It lengthens the life span and eliminates anger. Helpful in court and legal matters, it is also a money stone. Carry it about with you or place it in the till to attract wealth. It is a good stone to use when your creative abilities or talents need directing.

Calcite
A major balancer of the body, this stone comes in every Chakra colour. It helps the body to remember what it was like when it was without illness, and go back there. Calcite is good for students of arts and sciences.

Use clear calcite for meditation and connection to the upper realms, pink for love rituals, green for money spells, blue for healing and orange for energy. This is a very useful stone.

The Crystal List

Carnelian

This stone increases physical energy and stimulates the sexual regions. It eliminates apathy and stimulates inquisitiveness. It helps us to eliminate negative emotions and benefits the study of the arts.

Celestite

This beautiful, blue crystal cluster brings about a feeling of inner peace. It creates calm and balance in times of despair, and love and light in times of pain.

Chrysoprase

This crystal helps banish greed and selfishness and can be used for protection and to attract money.

Citrine

Sometimes called the Merchant's Stone because in days gone by merchants would keep a piece of citrine in their moneybox to attract wealth.

Diamond

Known as a 'Girl's Best Friend' because it brings confidence to your emotions, and trust and fidelity to relationships. It fills the aura with healing light and attracts abundance into your life.

Emerald

This is a good stone to use when dealing with legal or business issues.

The Crystal List

Fluorite
This is effective for all health problems and helps to bring order to chaos. Place a piece on your computer and help to eliminate negative energy.

Garnet
Helps to heal mental, physical, emotional and spiritual systems.

Hematite
I cannot wear this as I find that I become very depressed. However, do not be put off by my experience as it may help you achieve greater heights than you think possible.

Herkimer Diamonds
Another of my favourites — a pure, clear stone that can be programmed to dispel negativity and promote love and harmony.

Jade
The Warriors Stone so called because it was worn in the breastplates of warriors and high priests. It is best used for protection and challenging situations.

Jasper
A calming stone that promotes friendship and sharing.

Labradorite
Containing the energy of both the sun and the moon,

this stone is a great healer as well as being beautiful to look at and comfortable to wear.

Lapis Lazuli
The success giver, this beautiful blue stone is a major healer and will help to eliminate depression and introduce joy.

Malachite
The stone of communication, music and courage also has the ability to enhance your immune system.

Moldavite
This is a very special stone that does not come from the planet earth. It will come to you when you need it and will suit any purpose.

Magical in its appearance and properties, it is a joy to own and wear even if only for a short time.

Moonstone
This will help to enhance femininity in women and will balance the menstrual cycle, and for men it will help them understand their feminine side and be more caring towards the female sex.

Obsidian, black
The most common grounding stone. It should be used with care as too much can bring depression.

Obsidian, snowflake

This unusual looking crystal can ward off and protect you from the negative attitudes and energy of others. It helps to bring repressed feelings gently to the surface.

Pearl

This beautiful stone symbolises all that is pure. It is calming and soothing and aids fertility.

Pyrite

Known as Fool's Gold, this bright crystal will draw good positive energy to you and help to bring brightness into your life.

Rose Quartz

The Stone of Love helps you to draw love toward you, promotess self-love and eases heartache.

Ruby

This crystal aids concentration and brings protection.

Rutile

The fine lines in this crystal are sometimes known as Angel's Hair. This is another of my favourites and it is a very powerful crystal, which is beautiful as well as interesting to look at.

Smoky Quartzostone brings protection and harmony and is a good all round healer and balancer.

Numbers

Zero You are in between the end of your old cycle and the beginning of a new one. Be confident and make any necessary changes.

One The number of leadership, new beginnings, new ideas and inspiration. Exciting new changes lie ahead.

Two The number of tact and diplomacy, balance and harmony. Be prepared for some surprises.

Three The number of pregnancy, nursing or nurturing, socializing and having good times with friends. It indicates clubs, societies, organisations and also the countryside.

Four The number of security, assets and the home. Repairs, renovations and renewals may be expected around the home.

Five The number that shows the problem areas in your life, or any conflict that will be experienced. It is also linked with uniforms of any description and keys.

Six The number of tenderness, compassion, difficult choices, that have to be made, crossroads being reached and the eternal triangle. However, where five shows the problems, six is the number that provides the solutions.

Seven The number of control. This cannot be obtained

without full knowledge of all facts surrounding you. With inner questioning, you can then resume control in your life.

Eight The number of strength, determination and stubbornness.

Nine The number of completion and seeing the light at the end of the tunnel or finding your way after stumbling around in the dark. It shows difficult tasks being completed.